the Entertaining COOKBOOK

the Entertaining COOKBOOK

SOUTHERN LADY'S BEST TABLES, RECIPES & PARTY MENUS

VOLUME I

hm | books

hm | books

EXECUTIVE VICE PRESIDENT/CCO Brian K. Hoffman
VICE PRESIDENT/EDITORIAL Cindy Smith Cooper
ART DIRECTOR Tracy Wood-Franklin
COPY EDITOR Terri Robertson

SOUTHERN LADY EDITORIAL

EDITOR Andrea Fanning
CREATIVE DIRECTOR/PHOTOGRAPHY Mac Jamieson
ART DIRECTOR Amy Robinson
ASSOCIATE EDITOR Karen Pruitt Callaway
ASSISTANT EDITOR Kathleen Johnston Whaley
EDITORIAL ASSISTANT Becky Goff
CONTRIBUTING COPY EDITOR Donna Baldone
CONTRIBUTING WRITER Lauren Rippey Eberle
STYLISTS Adrienne Alldredge Williams,
Yukie McLean
SENIOR PHOTOGRAPHERS Marcy Black Simpson,
John O'Hagan
PHOTOGRAPHERS William Dickey,
Stephanie Welbourne Grund, Sarah Swihart,
Kamin Williams
CONTRIBUTING PHOTOGRAPHER
Kimberly Finkel Davis
SENIOR DIGITAL IMAGING SPECIALIST
Delisa McDaniel
DIGITAL IMAGING SPECIALIST Clark Densmore

hm
hoffmanmedia

PRESIDENT Phyllis Hoffman DePiano
EXECUTIVE VICE PRESIDENT/COO Eric W. Hoffman
EXECUTIVE VICE PRESIDENT/CCO Brian K. Hoffman
EXECUTIVE VICE PRESIDENT/CFO G. Marc Neas
VICE PRESIDENT/MANUFACTURING Greg Baugh
VICE PRESIDENT/EDITORIAL Cindy Smith Cooper
VICE PRESIDENT/PRODUCT & BRAND DEVELOPMENT
Jennifer Sharpton Jaquess
VICE PRESIDENT/CONSUMER MARKETING Silvia Rider

Hoffman Media
1900 International Park Drive, Suite 50
Birmingham, Alabama 35243
www.hoffmanmedia.com

ISBN # 978-0-9770069-0-8

On the cover: Lemon-Raspberry Pound Cake with Vanilla
Buttercream, page 210. Photography by Mac Jamieson.
Styling by Yukie McLean. Food styling by Loren Wood.

Contents

DINING AT HOME

SOIREE AWAY

BEST RECIPES

INTRODUCTION

In the South entertaining is an art form. From a beautiful flower arrangement that draws smiles of delight to layers of linens that perfectly complement cherished china patterns to crystal and silver that sparkles and shines, a well-appointed table is a lovely reflection of the hostess and her thoughtful hospitality. But when all is said and done, it's the food itself—every scrumptious dish—that truly defines the occasion.

For Southerners, any gathering is an excuse to serve food, and there's nothing we love more than gathering people around the table and sharing some of our favorite dishes. At *Southern Lady*, we have a treasure trove of tried-and-true recipes from the magazine that we rely on, but we have often wished that we had them all in one book rather than having to flip back through the issues or try to keep up with instructions scribbled on tiny cards. We are so pleased that our wish is now a beautifully bound reality.

So for those loyal readers who have longed for a compilation of our wonderful recipes—or for any home chef searching for fabulous new dishes to add to her repertoire—we are happy to present *Southern Lady*'s first volume of *The Entertaining Cookbook*. Enjoy!

DINING
AT HOME

DINNER
for Two

Show that someone special how much you care with a delectable meal that's perfectly sized for a pair. Whether for your valentine or your best friend, this appetizing fare will provide all you need for an unforgettable evening.

Menu

INDIVIDUAL BEEF WELLINGTONS WITH SHERRIED CREAM SAUCE

SAUTÉED GREEN BEANS WITH PECANS

SWISS-TARRAGON POTATOES

LEMON-RASPBERRY CHEESECAKES FOR TWO

Individual Beef Wellingtons

Makes 2 servings

2   (4-ounce) beef tenderloin
    fillets, 1 inch thick
1   clove garlic, minced
Salt and pepper
2   tablespoons butter
1   cup finely chopped fresh
    mushrooms
3   tablespoons minced shallot
1   tablespoon minced fresh parsley
2   tablespoons dry sherry
2   tablespoons heavy cream
½   (17.3-ounce) package frozen puff
    pastry sheets, thawed
1   large egg, lightly beaten
Sherried Cream Sauce
    (recipe follows)

1. Preheat oven to 425°.

2. Rub beef fillets with garlic, and season with salt and pepper to taste. In a heavy skillet, melt butter over medium heat; add beef, and cook for 3 minutes on each side or until browned. Remove from skillet, reserving pan drippings, and drain beef on paper towels.

3. Add mushrooms, shallots, parsley, sherry, and cream to pan drippings. Cook over medium heat until shallots are tender and all liquid is absorbed. Spread mushroom mixture evenly over each beef fillet.

4. On a lightly floured surface, unfold pastry sheet. Roll to ⅛-inch thickness, and cut into fourths.

5. Place each fillet, mushroom side down, in the center of a pastry square. Top with remaining squares, enclosing beef completely; crimp edges with fork to seal. If desired, roll out additional puff pastry, and cut out decorations, pressing lightly to top of crust.

6. Place beef on a baking sheet lined with parchment paper; brush with beaten egg. Bake for 15 to 20 minutes or until golden brown. Serve with Sherried Cream Sauce.

SHERRIED CREAM SAUCE

Makes 2 servings

1   tablespoon butter
2   shallots, chopped
½   cup sliced fresh mushrooms
1   tablespoon all-purpose flour
¼   cup sherry
6   ounces beef broth
Salt and pepper
¼   cup heavy cream

1. In a medium skillet, melt butter over medium heat. Cook shallots and mushrooms until tender; stir in flour. Gradually add sherry and broth; season with salt and pepper to taste. Reduce heat to low; simmer for 10 minutes. Stir in cream, and simmer for 5 more minutes.

Sautéed Green Beans with Pecans

Makes 2 servings

3   tablespoons olive oil
½   pound frozen cut green beans
½   teaspoon sugar
½   teaspoon salt
¼   teaspoon ground black pepper
3   tablespoons teriyaki sauce
2   tablespoons butter
¼   cup chopped pecans

1. In a large skillet, heat oil over medium-high heat. Add beans to skillet, and cook, stirring occasionally, until lightly browned. Add sugar, salt, pepper, and teriyaki sauce; cook for 2 to 3 minutes. Add butter, stirring until butter melts. Stir in pecans. Cook for 2 to 3 minutes.

Swiss-Tarragon Potatoes

Makes 2 servings

4   small Yukon gold potatoes,
    peeled and very thinly sliced
¼   cup heavy cream
1   teaspoon salt
½   teaspoon ground black pepper
1   teaspoon butter, softened
1   cup grated Swiss cheese
2   tablespoons minced fresh tarragon

1. Preheat oven to 400°. In a small bowl, combine potatoes, cream, salt, and pepper, tossing gently to coat. Coat 2 (4x2-inch) ramekins with butter. Divide one-third of potato mixture between ramekins. Top each with 2½ tablespoons cheese and 1 teaspoon tarragon. Repeat layers twice.

2. Bake for 30 minutes. Remove from oven, and let stand for 5 minutes. Run a knife around edges of ramekins. Invert ramekins onto plates. Garnish with fresh tarragon, if desired.

Lemon-Raspberry Cheesecakes for Two

Makes 2 servings

Crust:
½ cup crushed vanilla wafers
2 tablespoons sugar
2 tablespoons butter, melted

Filling:
12 ounces cream cheese, softened
6 tablespoons sugar
1 large egg
1 egg yolk
½ cup sour cream
2 tablespoons all-purpose flour
½ teaspoon vanilla extract
2 teaspoons lemon zest
2 tablespoons fresh lemon juice

Raspberry sauce:
1 cup frozen raspberries, thawed
⅓ cup sugar
½ teaspoon lemon zest
1 tablespoon water

Sour cream sauce:
½ cup sour cream
2 tablespoons sugar
1 to 2 tablespoons water

1. Preheat oven to 300°.

2. To prepare crust: Combine wafers, sugar, and butter. Press crust in bottoms of 2 (4½-inch) mini springform pans. Bake for 8 to 10 minutes or until golden.

3. To prepare filling: In a medium bowl, beat cream cheese and sugar at medium speed with an electric mixer until creamy. Add egg and egg yolk, beating well. Add sour cream, flour, vanilla, lemon zest, and lemon juice, stirring until well combined. Pour half of batter into each prepared crust.

4. Bake for 40 to 45 minutes or until centers are almost set. Remove from oven. Cool completely at room temperature (up to 2 hours), and chill.

5. To prepare raspberry sauce: Puree raspberries in blender. In a small saucepan, combine raspberry puree, sugar, lemon zest, and water; bring to a boil over medium heat, reduce heat, and simmer for 5 minutes. Pour sauce through a sieve, discarding seeds, if desired. Cool completely.

6. To prepare sour cream sauce: Combine sour cream, sugar, and 1 tablespoon water, stirring until smooth. Add additional water, if necessary, to reach desired consistency.

7. Run a knife around edges of cheesecakes to loosen from sides of pans, and remove from pans. Serve with raspberry sauce and sour cream sauce (see Easy Decorating Technique below).

Everyday Gourmet: EASY DECORATING TECHNIQUE

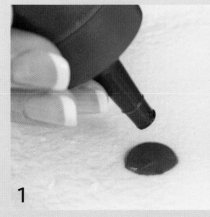

1   **2**   **3**

1. Using a squeeze bottle, pipe a ¼-inch diameter dot of raspberry sauce onto cheesecake. **2.** With a separate squeeze bottle, pipe a smaller dot of cream sauce slightly above the center of the raspberry dot. **3.** Starting just outside the raspberry dot, drag a toothpick through the center of both dots and through the other side, forming a point at the end. If necessary, repeat process to define shape. **Note:** For best results, both sauces should be at room temperature. Before you begin, practice on waxed paper. Have fun perfecting the technique—try dragging the toothpick at different speeds and at various angles. Be sure you're comfortable with the results before moving to the actual dessert for presentation.

Time to TOAST

Celebrate New Year's Day—or any special occasion—with a champagne brunch that brings together the best of friends for the best of times.

Menu

EGGS BENEDICT WITH HOLLANDAISE SAUCE

APPLE BUTTER MUFFINS

CHAMPAGNE FRUIT SALAD

MIMOSA

MOCK CHAMPAGNE COCKTAIL

Mock Champagne Cocktail

Makes 4 servings

1½   cups sparkling white grape juice, chilled
1½   cups apple juice, chilled
1   tablespoon fresh lemon juice
Garnish: fresh raspberries

1. Combine white grape juice, apple juice, and lemon juice. Pour into champagne flutes. Garnish with fresh raspberries, if desired.

Mimosa

Makes 4 servings

1⅓   cups orange juice, chilled
2   teaspoons orange liqueur
1   cup champagne or sparkling wine, chilled
Garnish: fresh raspberries

1. Combine orange juice and orange liqueur. Pour into champagne flutes; top with champagne. Garnish with fresh raspberries, if desired.

Champagne Fruit Salad

Makes 4 servings

½   cup strawberry syrup
⅓   cup fresh orange juice
1   tablespoon honey
½   teaspoon orange zest
4   large oranges, peeled and sectioned
1   (1-pound) container fresh strawberries, sliced
½   cup champagne
Garnish: fresh mint leaves

1. In a small saucepan, combine strawberry syrup, orange juice, honey, and orange zest over medium heat. Bring to a simmer, and cook for 5 minutes, stirring occasionally, until sauce thickens slightly.

2. Remove from heat, and cool for 10 minutes; pour over fruit. Cover and refrigerate for 1 hour.

3. To serve, pour champagne over fruit mixture; stir gently. Garnish with fresh mint leaves, if desired.

The laughter will flow as freely as the conversation at a divine New Year's Day brunch, where the menu offerings are as special as the occasion itself. Thoughtful place cards penned by the hostess are always sure to inspire plenty of smiles around the table.

Eggs Benedict
Makes 4 servings

12	cups water
2	tablespoons white vinegar
1	tablespoon salt
4	English muffins, split
¼	cup butter, melted
8	large eggs
8	slices Canadian bacon

Hollandaise Sauce (recipe follows)
Garnish: chopped tomato,
  fresh thyme, freshly ground
  black pepper

1. In a large Dutch oven, combine water, vinegar, and salt over medium-low heat. Bring to a gentle simmer.

2. Preheat oven to 500°; place oven rack in center position. Brush cut sides of English muffin halves with butter. Place, cut sides up, on a baking sheet, and set aside.

3. Cooking 4 eggs at a time, break each egg into a saucer, and carefully slide against edge of pan into simmering water. Simmer for 5 minutes or until whites are set and yolks are still soft. Gently remove eggs from pan with slotted spoon, and drain on paper towels; repeat with remaining eggs. For best appearance, trim ragged edges with a sharp knife.

4. While eggs poach, bake English muffins for 3 minutes. Remove from oven, and top each muffin half with a slice of Canadian bacon. Return to oven, and bake for 3 to 4 minutes or until edges are lightly browned.

5. Place poached eggs on top of Canadian bacon; top with Hollandaise Sauce. Garnish with chopped tomato, fresh thyme, and freshly ground black pepper, if desired.

HOLLANDAISE SAUCE
Makes about 1¼ cups

4	egg yolks
1½	tablespoons fresh lemon juice
½	teaspoon Dijon mustard
⅛	teaspoon Worcestershire sauce
⅛	teaspoon hot sauce
1	cup butter, melted
2	tablespoons hot water
½	teaspoon salt
⅛	teaspoon ground white pepper

1. Fill bottom of double boiler with 1 inch of water. Bring water to a simmer over medium-low heat. Place top of double boiler over simmering water.

2. In top of double boiler, whisk together egg yolks, lemon juice, mustard, Worcestershire sauce, and hot sauce.

3. Whisking constantly, add melted butter, 2 tablespoons at a time, until all butter is incorporated. Whisk in water, as needed, to prevent sauce from becoming too thick.

4. Remove from heat, and whisk in salt and white pepper. Serve immediately.

Apple Butter Muffins
Makes 2 dozen

1¾	cups self-rising flour
½	cup sugar
½	teaspoon ground cinnamon
½	cup finely chopped apple
¾	cup buttermilk
½	cup apple butter
½	cup unsalted butter, melted
1	large egg, lightly beaten
¼	cup finely chopped apple cinnamon-glazed walnuts and almonds*

1. Preheat oven to 350°. Lightly grease a 24-cup mini muffin pan; set aside.

2. In a medium bowl, combine flour, sugar, and cinnamon. Stir in apple.

3. In a separate bowl, combine buttermilk, apple butter, melted butter, and egg. Add buttermilk mixture to flour mixture, stirring just until dry ingredients are moistened.

4. Spoon batter into prepared muffin cups. Top with chopped nuts. Bake for 23 to 25 minutes or until a wooden pick inserted in center comes out clean. Let cool in pan for 5 minutes before removing. Serve with additional apple butter, if desired.

*For testing purposes, we used Emerald Apple Cinnamon Glazed Walnuts 'n Almonds. Plain walnuts may be substituted.

FOR MY
Valentine

The romantic glow of candlelight and soft strains of Sinatra set the stage for an intimate dinner for two.

Menu

CREAMY VEGETABLE SOUP

STUFFED FILET MIGNON WITH MUSHROOM SAUCE

PARMESAN POLENTA CAKES

TRICOLORED VEGETABLES

FLOURLESS CHOCOLATE CAKE FOR TWO

Though a lasting love knows no boundaries of time, a heart can't help the blissful beating that comes from celebrating St. Valentine's Day. The occasion calls for something special—a table laden with rich expressions of romance. Glittering gold and passionate crimson paired with scrolled chairs and lavish pillows accent this spread that will make your dearest feel like the king of the castle—and your heart.

Creamy Vegetable Soup

Makes 3 cups

2	tablespoons butter
1	tablespoon olive oil
¾	cup finely chopped onion
½	cup finely chopped celery
½	cup finely chopped carrot
½	cup niblet corn
¼	teaspoon salt
¼	teaspoon ground black pepper
⅛	teaspoon garlic powder
2	tablespoons all-purpose flour
2	cups chicken broth
½	cup heavy whipping cream

Garnish: chopped celery, chopped carrot, fresh parsley

1. In a medium saucepan, melt butter with olive oil over medium heat. Add onion, celery, carrot, and corn. Cook for 8 minutes, stirring frequently, until vegetables are tender.

2. Add salt, pepper, and garlic powder, stirring until well combined. Add flour, and cook for 2 minutes, stirring constantly. Gradually stir in chicken broth. Bring to a simmer, stirring occasionally. Add cream, and cook for 5 to 10 minutes or until soup thickens slightly.

3. Garnish each serving with chopped celery, chopped carrot, and fresh parsley, if desired.

Parmesan Polenta Cakes
Makes 4 servings

3½ cups milk
¾   teaspoon salt
½   teaspoon ground black pepper
1   cup stone-ground yellow cornmeal
½   cup grated Parmigiano-Reggiano cheese
2   tablespoons butter
Garnish: shaved Parmigiano-Reggiano cheese, fresh basil leaves

1. Line bottom of a 9x5-inch loaf pan with waxed paper.

2. In a medium saucepan, combine milk, salt, and pepper; carefully bring to a boil over medium heat, stirring frequently. Gradually whisk in cornmeal. Reduce heat to low, cover, and cook for 30 minutes, stirring frequently. Add grated cheese, stirring until cheese melts. Cool slightly, and spread evenly in prepared pan; chill for 1 to 2 hours or until set. Remove from pan, and cut into fourths.

3. In a large nonstick skillet, melt butter over medium heat. Cook polenta squares for 2 minutes on each side or until golden brown. Garnish with shaved cheese and basil, if desired.

Tricolored Vegetables
Makes 2 to 4 servings

2   carrots, cut into ¼-inch strips
2   tablespoons butter
2   tablespoons olive oil
1   yellow bell pepper, cut into ¼-inch strips
1   (8-ounce) bag fresh sugar snap peas (about 2 cups)
½   teaspoon minced garlic
½   teaspoon salt
¼   teaspoon ground black pepper

1. In a small pot of boiling water, blanch carrots for 2 minutes; drain.

2. In a medium skillet, melt butter with oil over medium-high heat. Add carrots, bell pepper, and peas; sauté for 4 to 5 minutes or until crisp-tender. Add garlic, salt, and pepper, and sauté for 1 minute.

Stuffed Filet Mignon with Mushroom Sauce
Makes 2 servings

4   ounces cream cheese, softened
½   cup grated Parmigiano-Reggiano cheese
½   teaspoon minced garlic
1½ teaspoons chopped fresh basil
2   (8-ounce) beef tenderloin steaks
3   tablespoons olive oil
1   cup sliced baby bella mushrooms
1   teaspoon minced garlic
½   cup merlot or dry red wine
¼   cup beef broth
⅛   teaspoon ground black pepper
1   tablespoon butter

1. Preheat oven to 400°. Line a rimmed baking sheet with parchment paper.

2. In a small bowl, combine cream cheese, cheese, garlic, and basil. Cut a pocket into side of each steak. Spoon cheese mixture evenly into steak pockets.

3. In a large skillet, heat olive oil over medium heat. Cook steaks for 2 to 3 minutes on each side or until browned. Remove steaks, reserving drippings in pan, and place on prepared baking sheet. Bake for 15 to 20 minutes or until desired degree of doneness. Let steaks rest for 2 minutes. Spoon any melted cheese mixture back into pockets before serving.

4. Add mushrooms to drippings in pan, and cook for 2 minutes. Add garlic, and cook for 1 minute. Add wine; cook for 3 to 5 minutes or until most of liquid evaporates. Add beef broth and pepper, and cook for 1 minute. Remove from heat, and stir in butter. Spoon sauce over steaks.

Flourless Chocolate Cake for Two
Makes 1 (6-inch) cake

½   cup semisweet chocolate morsels
6   tablespoons butter
3   large eggs, separated
1   teaspoon vanilla extract
½   cup sugar
1   tablespoon unsweetened cocoa
     powder
⅛   teaspoon salt
½   cup hot fudge topping
Garnish: whipped cream, chocolate
     curls, fresh strawberries
     (see One Cake, Two Ways below)

1. Preheat oven to 325°. Fill an 8x8-inch baking pan with 1 inch of hot water; place in oven. Spray a 6-inch round cake pan with nonstick baking spray with flour. Line bottom with parchment paper; set aside.

2. In a small microwave-safe bowl, microwave chocolate and butter on High in 30-second intervals, stirring after each, until melted and smooth (about 1½ minutes total). Let cool slightly.

3. In a medium bowl, whisk together egg yolks and vanilla. Add chocolate mixture, whisking until smooth.

4. In a separate bowl, combine sugar, cocoa, and salt. Add to chocolate mixture, stirring until well combined.

5. In a separate bowl, beat egg whites at medium speed with an electric mixer until soft peaks form. Fold egg whites, one-third at a time, into chocolate mixture. Spoon batter into prepared 6-inch pan. Place in oven in center of 8x8-inch pan.

6. Bake for 50 to 55 minutes or until a wooden pick inserted in center comes out clean. Remove cake from water bath; cool in pan on wire rack for 10 minutes; remove from pan, and cool completely on wire rack.

7. Warm hot fudge topping according to package directions; spoon over cake. Garnish with whipped cream, chocolate curls, and strawberries, if desired.

One Cake, Two Ways

Step up the style of our basic chocolate cake by substituting homemade Orange Crème Anglaise for the store-bought fudge sauce. Garnish the decadent confection with edible gold, and serve with gold-dusted crème anglaise, fanned strawberries, and orange zest, as shown in the photo above.

ORANGE CRÈME ANGLAISE
Makes about 1 cup

3   egg yolks
¼   cup sugar
1   cup milk
1½   teaspoons orange zest
1   teaspoon orange-flavored liqueur
½   teaspoon vanilla extract

1. In a small bowl, combine egg yolks and sugar; beat at medium speed with an electric mixer for 2 minutes or until pale yellow in color; set aside.

2. In a medium saucepan, combine milk and zest. Bring to a simmer over medium heat (do not boil). Remove from heat.

3. Whisking constantly, add ½ cup milk mixture to yolk mixture. Add yolk mixture to remaining milk mixture in pan, whisking constantly. Cook over medium heat, whisking constantly, until mixture thickens, about 5 minutes. Remove from heat. Place saucepan in an ice-water bath. Stir in liqueur and vanilla. Stir sauce occasionally as it cools.

Sisterhood LUNCHEON

Set the table with your best china and linens for an elegant luncheon in honor of all the special Southern ladies in your life.

Menu

CREAMY CUCUMBER SOUP

MESCLUN SALAD WITH LEMON VINAIGRETTE

CHICKEN, MUSHROOM, AND SWISS QUICHE

ROSEMARY ROLLS

COCONUT MOUSSE

Creamy Cucumber Soup

Makes 6 to 8 servings

4   cucumbers, peeled, seeded, and coarsely chopped
6   green onions, chopped
2   tablespoons chopped fresh parsley
2   teaspoons chopped fresh dill
¼   cup lemon juice
1½   teaspoons salt
¾   teaspoon ground black pepper
2   cups buttermilk
½   cup sour cream
2   cups heavy cream
Garnish: sour cream, fresh dill

1. In a large bowl, combine all ingredients (except garnish). Process cucumber mixture, in batches, in a blender or food processor until smooth, stopping to scrape down sides.

2. Cover and chill for at least 4 hours or overnight. Garnish with sour cream and fresh dill, if desired.

Rosemary Rolls

Makes 1 dozen

¼   cup butter, softened
2   cups self-rising flour
1   cup milk
3   tablespoons mayonnaise
2   tablespoons sour cream
2   tablespoons chopped fresh rosemary
¼   teaspoon freshly ground black pepper

1. Preheat oven to 400°.

2. Generously grease each cup of a 12-cup muffin pan with butter.

3. In a medium bowl, combine flour, milk, mayonnaise, sour cream, rosemary, and pepper, stirring well. Spoon batter into muffin cups, filling halfway full.

4. Bake for 20 to 30 minutes or until golden brown.

From your longtime best friend to your cherished grandmother, each "sister" has had a profound impact on your life in one way or another. Host a gathering in honor of these lovely ladies and the bonds you share. Fill the guest list with absolute royalty—the aunt who offered plenty of encouragement and sound advice; the college roommate, with whom you shared hilarious moments and memorable road trips; your mother, whose embrace still feels like home no matter where you live; and your actual sister, who is never more than a phone call away. Next, set a delicious spread, and dedicate the entire day to sisterhood. This dazzling luncheon menu is sure to express to the honorees your appreciation for all that they've done and all that they do.

Mesclun Salad with Lemon Vinaigrette

Makes 6 servings

1   package mesclun greens, washed
    and dried
½   head of radicchio, chopped
1   pint grape tomatoes, halved
    lengthwise
Lemon Vinaigrette (recipe follows)
Garnish: shaved Parmigiano-Reggiano
    cheese, toasted almonds

1. In a medium bowl, combine mesclun greens, radicchio, and grape tomatoes. Gradually add just enough Lemon Vinaigrette to coat greens, tossing gently.

2. Garnish with shaved Parmigiano-Reggiano cheese and toasted almonds, if desired. Serve with remaining vinaigrette on the side.

LEMON VINAIGRETTE
Makes about 1½ cups

⅓   cup lemon juice
1   tablespoon Dijon mustard
2   tablespoons sugar
¼   teaspoon salt
¼   teaspoon ground black pepper
1   cup vegetable oil

1. In a small bowl, combine juice, mustard, sugar, salt, and pepper. Slowly whisk in oil. Cover and chill. Whisk before using.

Chicken, Mushroom, and Swiss Quiche

Makes 6 servings

½   (14.1-ounce) package refrigerated
    pie crust
2   tablespoons butter
2   tablespoons olive oil
2   cloves garlic, minced
½   cup diced onion
1   cup sliced fresh mushrooms
2   boneless skinless chicken breasts,
    diced
3   large eggs
1   cup half-and-half
½   teaspoon dry mustard
½   teaspoon salt
¼   teaspoon ground black pepper
1½ cups grated Swiss cheese, divided

1. Preheat oven to 450°.

2. Unroll pie crust on a lightly floured surface. Roll into a 12-inch circle. Fit into a 9-inch deep-dish pie plate; fold edges under, and crimp. Prick bottom and sides of crust with a fork. Bake for 6 to 8 minutes. Remove from oven; set aside.

3. Reduce oven temperature to 375°. In a large skillet, melt butter with olive oil over medium-high heat. Add garlic, onion, and mushrooms; sauté until tender. With a slotted spoon, remove vegetables to a bowl, reserving oil in pan.

4. Add diced chicken to pan, and cook, stirring frequently, until lightly browned. Remove chicken from pan, and set aside.

5. In a small bowl, whisk together eggs, half-and-half, dry mustard, salt, and pepper.

6. To assemble quiche, sprinkle 1 cup cheese in prepared crust. Layer chicken and vegetable mixture over cheese. Pour egg mixture over chicken and vegetables. Top with remaining ½ cup cheese. Bake for 30 minutes or until middle is set. Cool for 10 to 15 minutes before serving.

HOW TO CREATE A
Lemon Tree Centerpiece

1. Start with a Styrofoam cone and, using florist picks, attach lemons in concentric circles.
2. Place a lemon on top of cone.
3. Fill in empty places with sprigs of boxwood or other greenery until all Styrofoam is covered.
Tip: Because the finished project will be heavy, construct the tree in or close to the place where you want to display it.

Coconut Mousse
Makes 6 to 8 servings

¼ cup butter, softened
1 (8-ounce) package cream cheese, softened
¾ cup sugar
½ cup cream of coconut
½ teaspoon vanilla or almond extract
1¾ cups heavy whipping cream
½ cup sweetened flaked coconut
Garnish: toasted coconut

1. In a large bowl, beat butter and cream cheese at medium speed with an electric mixer until creamy. Add sugar, cream of coconut, and vanilla or almond extract, beating well. With mixer running, gradually add cream, beating until stiff peaks form. Gently fold in coconut. Cover and chill until ready to serve.

2. Spoon mousse into glasses. Garnish with toasted coconut, if desired.

35

Celebrating MOTHERS

Commemorate Mother's Day with a splendid tea as feminine and elegant as these cherished ladies. Draw inspiration from the garden to infuse this very special occasion with a lovely floral theme.

Menu

LAVENDER SCONES WITH STRAWBERRY DEVONSHIRE CREAM

CALLA LILY TEA SANDWICHES

RASPBERRY-WHITE CHOCOLATE TARTLETS

A mother's love is like no other love. It lifts us up and keeps us grounded. It teaches us to take pride in our accomplishments but also to be humble. It encourages us to laugh with abandon, and it tenderly dries our tears, too. It's no wonder that we set aside a day each May to honor the wonderful women who have given us unconditional and immeasurable love since our beginning breaths.

For this celebration, nothing but the best will do. A beautiful peaches-and-cream color scheme sets the stage for a queen-worthy tea. Inspired by floral offerings from the garden, the menu offers a scrumptious spread of tea sandwiches, tarts, and scones. Each tiny detail— rosebud sugar cubes, dainty china accented with gold, embroidered linen napkins— reminds us of the loving care our mothers lavished on us.

Lavender Scones
Makes 16 scones

2½   cups all-purpose flour
⅓   cup plus 2 tablespoons sugar, divided
1½   teaspoons baking powder
½   teaspoon salt
½   cup butter, cut into pieces
2   tablespoons dried lavender
¾   cup plus 1 tablespoon heavy whipping cream, divided

1. Preheat oven to 375°. Line a baking sheet with parchment paper.

2. In a large bowl, combine flour, ⅓ cup sugar, baking powder, and salt. Using a pastry blender, cut butter into flour mixture until crumbly. Add lavender; mix well. Add ¾ cup cream, stirring just until dry ingredients are moistened.

3. On a lightly floured surface, roll dough to ½-inch thickness. Using a 2-inch round cutter, cut scones, and place on prepared baking sheet. Brush scones with remaining 1 tablespoon cream, and sprinkle with remaining 2 tablespoons sugar. Bake for 14 to 16 minutes or until lightly browned.

STRAWBERRY DEVONSHIRE CREAM
Makes about 2 cups

1   (8-ounce) package cream cheese, softened
½   cup sour cream
1   tablespoon strawberry extract
½   teaspoon vanilla extract
½   cup heavy whipping cream
¼   cup confectioners' sugar

1. In a medium bowl, combine cream cheese, sour cream, strawberry extract, and vanilla. Beat at medium speed with an electric mixer until well combined.

2. In a separate bowl, beat cream until soft peaks form. Add sugar, and beat until stiff peaks form. Fold whipped cream mixture into cream cheese mixture. Cover and chill.

41

Calla Lily Tea Sandwiches

Makes about 4 dozen

1   (5.2-ounce) package garlic-and-herbs Boursin cheese, softened
1   (3-ounce) package cream cheese, softened
¼   cup finely chopped toasted walnuts
⅛   teaspoon ground red pepper
⅛   teaspoon ground black pepper
48 slices white bread
Paprika
2   carrots, peeled
Garnish: green onions

1. In a small bowl, combine Boursin cheese, cream cheese, walnuts, red pepper, and black pepper. Beat at medium speed with an electric mixer until creamy.

2. Using a 2½-inch cutter, cut 48 rounds from bread. With a rolling pin, roll each bread round to ⅛-inch thickness.

3. Spread approximately 1 teaspoon cream cheese mixture on each bread round. Sprinkle center with paprika, and fold bottom of prepared bread round over, pinching end to seal.

4. Cut small pieces of carrot, and place in center of each sandwich for flower stamen. Garnish with green onion tops to form stems, if desired.

Sugared Flowers

Sparkling flowers are so pretty on dessert plates. To make your own, lightly beat one egg white in a small bowl. Choose thin-petaled flowers—such as roses, geraniums, or violets—and, using a new paintbrush, coat each petal with egg white. Sprinkle superfine sugar over flowers, and gently shake off excess. Let dry on waxed paper. If necessary, granulated sugar can be ground in the food processor and substituted for the superfine variety.

Raspberry-White Chocolate Tartlets

Makes 2 dozen

3   cups crushed shortbread cookies
1¼ cups very finely chopped honey-roasted macadamia nuts
¼   cup plus 1 tablespoon sugar, divided
3   tablespoons butter, melted
1   egg white, lightly beaten
2   tablespoons cold water
1   teaspoon unflavored gelatin
1   (3-ounce) package cream cheese, softened
2   tablespoons unsalted butter, softened
3   tablespoons seedless raspberry preserves, melted
1   teaspoon raspberry extract
½   cup confectioners' sugar
¾   cup heavy whipping cream
⅓   cup finely chopped white chocolate
Garnish: fresh raspberries, pink sugar, fresh mint leaves

1. Preheat oven to 350°. In a medium bowl, combine cookie crumbs, macadamia nuts, ¼ cup sugar, and melted butter. Add egg white, stirring until well combined. Press crumb mixture into bottom and three-fourths up sides of 2 (12-cup) mini cheesecake pans. Bake for 10 minutes. Cool completely in pan.

2. In a small microwave-safe bowl, combine water and gelatin; let stand for 5 minutes. Microwave on High until gelatin dissolves (about 15 seconds); cool slightly.

3. In a medium bowl, combine cream cheese, butter, melted raspberry preserves, and raspberry extract. Beat at medium speed with an electric mixer until creamy. Add confectioners' sugar, beating until well combined.

4. In a separate bowl, beat cream and remaining 1 tablespoon sugar at high speed until soft peaks form. Add gelatin mixture, beating until stiff peaks form. Fold whipped cream mixture into cream cheese mixture. Fold in white chocolate.

5. Spoon or pipe mixture into prepared crusts; cover and chill for 1 to 2 hours. Remove tartlets from pans. Garnish with fresh raspberries, pink sugar, and fresh mint, if desired.

FRESH
& Delicious

Vine-ripened strawberries, sweet honeydew, tangy kiwi—summer offers such luscious delights! Gather these goodies to create fruit-filled desserts as fresh and cool as a soft summer breeze.

Menu

FRESH FRUIT TARTS

SEVEN-LAYER FRUIT SALAD

STRAWBERRY SHORTCAKE
WITH AMARETTO CREAM

Fresh Fruit Tarts

Makes 1 dozen

1   (14.1-ounce) package refrigerated pie crusts
2   (8-ounce) packages cream cheese, softened
¼   cup plus 2 tablespoons honey, divided
2   tablespoons lemon zest
2   tablespoons fresh lemon juice
½   cup confectioners' sugar
1   (1-pound) container fresh strawberries, sliced
4   kiwifruit, peeled and sliced into quarters
1   cup fresh blueberries
1   cup fresh raspberries

1. Preheat oven to 450°.

2. On lightly floured surface, unroll crusts. Using a 4½-inch round cutter, cut 6 circles from each pie crust. Line 12 (4-inch) tart pans with prepared crusts; prick bottom of crusts with fork. Place on a baking sheet, and bake for 7 to 8 minutes or until golden brown. Cool on wire racks for 5 minutes; remove from pans, and cool completely.

3. In a medium bowl, combine cream cheese, ¼ cup honey, lemon zest, and lemon juice. Beat at medium speed with an electric mixer until creamy. Add confectioners' sugar, beating until combined.

4. Spoon cream cheese mixture into prepared crusts. Top with strawberries, kiwifruit, blueberries, and raspberries.

5. In a small microwave-safe bowl, microwave remaining 2 tablespoons honey on High for 15 seconds or until melted. Using a small pastry brush, brush honey over tarts.

Strawberry Shortcake

Makes 8 servings

1   cup butter, softened
2   cups sugar
5   large eggs
1   tablespoon strawberry extract
½   teaspoon vanilla extract
2¼ cups all-purpose flour
½   teaspoon salt
½   cup sour cream
1   cup chopped fresh strawberries
1   (1-pound) container strawberries, sliced
½   cup strawberry syrup
Amaretto Cream (recipe follows)
Garnish: toasted chopped almonds, fresh mint sprigs

1. Preheat oven to 350°. Grease and flour a 10x5¼-inch loaf pan; set aside.

2. In a medium bowl, beat butter at medium speed with an electric mixer until creamy. Gradually add sugar, beating until fluffy. Add eggs, one at a time, beating well after each addition. Beat in strawberry extract and vanilla.

3. In a separate bowl, combine flour and salt; gradually add to butter mixture, beating just until combined. Stir in sour cream and chopped strawberries.

4. Spoon batter into prepared pan. Bake for 1 hour. Cover loosely with aluminum foil, and bake for 40 to 45 minutes longer or until a wooden pick inserted in center comes out clean. Cool cake in pan on a wire rack for 10 minutes; remove from pan, and cool completely.

5. Cut cake into squares, and top with sliced strawberries, strawberry syrup, and Amaretto Cream. Garnish with toasted chopped almonds and mint, if desired.

AMARETTO CREAM

Makes about 3 cups

1   cup heavy whipping cream
¼   cup sour cream
½   cup confectioners' sugar
3   tablespoons almond-flavored liqueur

1. In a medium bowl, combine cream and sour cream. Beat at medium-high speed with an electric mixer until soft peaks form. Add confectioners' sugar and almond-flavored liqueur, and beat until stiff peaks form. Cover and chill until ready to use.

Note: One teaspoon almond extract may be substituted for almond-flavored liqueur, if desired.

Seven-Layer Fruit Salad

Makes 10 to 12 servings

3   cups cubed cantaloupe
3   cups cubed fresh pineapple
3   cups sliced fresh strawberries
4   bananas, sliced
3   cups fresh blueberries
3   cups cubed honeydew
1   (12-ounce) container frozen nondairy whipped topping, thawed
1   (6-ounce) container strawberry yogurt
2   teaspoons strawberry extract
Garnish: fresh fruit

1. In a large salad bowl, layer cantaloupe, pineapple, strawberries, bananas, blueberries, and honeydew.

2. In a medium bowl, combine whipped topping, strawberry yogurt, and strawberry extract. Spoon whipped topping mixture over fruit. Garnish with additional fresh fruit, if desired.

Anniversary DINNER

Whether it's your first year of wedded bliss or your fortieth, say you'd marry him all over again with an anniversary meal just as wonderful as he is.

Menu

SEARED SCALLOP SALAD
WITH CORN RELISH AND
FRESH BASIL VINAIGRETTE

SHRIMP RISOTTO

MARINATED ROASTED
ASPARAGUS

STRAWBERRIES AND CREAM

SWEETHEART
CHAMPAGNE COCKTAIL

Y You think his gray hair looks distinguished; he still calls you his "girl." And though it has been ages since you walked down the aisle, the love you felt then has grown deeper with every passing moment. To celebrate another year of wedded bliss, serve a sensational meal in simple surroundings.

Seared Scallop Salad with Corn Relish

Makes 2 servings

1   tablespoon butter
½   cup fresh corn kernels
2   tablespoons finely chopped red bell pepper
2   tablespoons finely chopped green bell pepper
2   tablespoons chopped shallot
1   teaspoon minced garlic
3   tablespoons heavy whipping cream
¼   teaspoon salt
⅛   teaspoon ground red pepper
2   tablespoons olive oil
6   large fresh sea scallops
4   cups mesclun greens
Fresh Basil Vinaigrette (recipe follows)
Garnish: fresh basil

1. In a small skillet, melt butter over medium heat. Add corn, bell pepper, shallot, and garlic. Cook for 4 to 5 minutes or until tender. Add cream, salt, and red pepper. Cook for 1 to 2 minutes, stirring frequently, until liquid evaporates. Remove from heat; cover to keep warm.

2. In a large nonstick skillet, heat oil over medium-high heat. Add scallops; cook for 2 to 3 minutes on each side or until golden brown.

3. To serve, toss mesclun greens with 3 tablespoons Fresh Basil Vinaigrette. Divide greens between two salad plates, and top each with 3 scallops and corn relish. Drizzle salads with additional vinaigrette. Garnish with fresh basil, if desired. Serve immediately.

FRESH BASIL VINAIGRETTE
Makes ¾ cup

½   cup chopped fresh basil
¼   cup fresh lemon juice
1   tablespoon Dijon mustard
1   teaspoon sugar
¼   teaspoon salt
¼   teaspoon ground black pepper
½   cup olive oil

1. In the container of an electric blender, combine basil, lemon juice, mustard, sugar, salt, and pepper. Process until blended. With blender running, add oil in a slow, steady stream; process until blended. Cover and chill. Whisk before using.

Sweetheart Champagne Cocktail

Makes 1 serving

1   tablespoon strawberry-flavored syrup
1   tablespoon almond-flavored liqueur
4   ounces chilled champagne
Garnish: fresh strawberry

1. Pour strawberry syrup into a chilled champagne flute. Add liqueur. Gently add champagne. Garnish with a strawberry, if desired. Stir gently to combine before drinking.

Marinated Roasted Asparagus

Makes 2 servings

- ¼   cup teriyaki sauce
- 2   tablespoons balsamic vinegar
- 2   tablespoons dark brown sugar
- 1   teaspoon minced garlic
- ¼   cup olive oil
- ½   pound fresh asparagus (thin spears), trimmed

1. In a small bowl, combine teriyaki sauce, vinegar, brown sugar, and garlic. Whisk mixture until sugar dissolves. Slowly add oil, whisking to combine. Place asparagus in a resealable plastic bag. Add teriyaki mixture. Seal bag, and marinate in refrigerator for 4 to 6 hours.

2. Preheat oven to 425°. Line a rimmed baking sheet with aluminum foil. Remove asparagus from bag, discarding marinade. Place asparagus on prepared baking sheet. Bake for 5 to 6 minutes.

Strawberries and Cream

Makes 2 servings

- 1   cup heavy whipping cream
- ¼   cup confectioners' sugar
- 2   tablespoons white-chocolate-flavored liqueur
- 1   cup diced fresh strawberries
- 1   cup chopped meringue cookies
- ¼   cup finely chopped white chocolate

Garnish: strawberries, white chocolate curls, meringue cookies

1. In a medium bowl, beat cream at high speed with an electric mixer until soft peaks form. Add confectioners' sugar and liqueur; beat until stiff peaks form. Fold in strawberries, meringue cookies, and white chocolate. Garnish with strawberries, white chocolate curls, and meringue cookies, if desired.

Shrimp Risotto

Makes 2 to 4 servings

- 4   tablespoons olive oil, divided
- 12   fresh jumbo shrimp, peeled and deveined
- 1   teaspoon minced garlic
- ¼   teaspoon salt
- ¼   teaspoon ground black pepper
- ¼   cup finely chopped onion
- 1   cup Arborio rice
- 4   cups hot chicken broth
- ¼   cup heavy whipping cream
- 2   tablespoons chopped green onion
- 1   teaspoon lemon zest
- ⅛   teaspoon ground white pepper
- ½   cup freshly grated Parmesan cheese
- 2   tablespoons butter

Garnish: chopped green onion, lemon zest

1. In a large saucepan, heat 2 tablespoons oil over medium-high heat. Add shrimp, garlic, salt, and black pepper; cook for 1 to 2 minutes or until shrimp are just pink. Remove shrimp to a bowl; set aside.

2. Reduce heat to medium. Add remaining 2 tablespoons oil to pan. Add onion, and cook for 1 minute, stirring frequently. Add rice; cook for 2 to 3 minutes or until very lightly browned, stirring frequently. Add hot broth, ¼ cup at a time, allowing liquid to be absorbed after each addition, stirring constantly. Repeat procedure until rice becomes creamy in texture, about 20 to 25 minutes.

3. Add cream, green onion, lemon zest, white pepper, and shrimp, stirring to combine. Remove from heat. Add cheese and butter; stir until cheese and butter melt. Garnish with chopped green onion and lemon zest, if desired.

Two for One

A classic dessert, Strawberries and Cream makes a light and luscious ending to any spring or summer meal. Made with store-bought meringue cookies and just five other simple ingredients, the confection can be created in an instant. For dinner parties or other special occasions, use this recipe to make mini trifles. Layer crumbles of your favorite pound cake, fresh-from-the-garden berries, and *Southern Lady's* Strawberries and Cream for a sweet finale that's as easy as it is elegant.

Tricks & TREATS

October brings thrills and chills and plenty of opportunities for little ones to play and pretend. Celebrate this candy-filled time of year with a dandy of a party sure to delight for hours on end.

Menu

HAUNTED HAYSTACKS

GHOULED CHEESE

SPOOKY SNACK MIX

CREEPY CRAWLER CUPCAKES

BREW-HAHA

Brew-haha
Makes about 1½ gallons

6   cups orange juice
6   cups pineapple juice
6   cups apple juice
1   (2-liter) bottle lemon-lime
     carbonated beverage, chilled
Garnish: small green apples

1. In a large container, combine orange juice, pineapple juice, and apple juice; stir until well combined. Cover and chill.

2. To serve, add lemon-lime carbonated beverage; stir gently. Garnish with small green apples, if desired.

Note: Add frozen grapes to the punch for extra fun.

Ghouled Cheese
Makes 1 dozen

12   slices white bread
2   cups finely shredded Cheddar
     cheese or Italian cheese blend
⅔   cup mayonnaise
½   teaspoon garlic powder
Decoration: sliced black olives

1. Preheat oven to 500°. Line a baking sheet with aluminum foil. Using cookie cutters, cut bread into desired shapes, such as pumpkins and ghosts.

2. In a medium bowl, stir together cheese, mayonnaise, and garlic powder. Spread over one side of bread shapes; decorate with olives. Place on prepared baking sheet; bake for 5 minutes.

Haunted Haystacks

Makes 1½ dozen

2   (4-ounce) bars white chocolate, chopped
1   (10-ounce) package peanut butter morsels
5   cups pretzel sticks, broken in half
18 candy pumpkins

1. In a medium microwave-safe bowl, microwave white chocolate and peanut butter morsels on High in 30-second intervals, stirring after each, until melted and smooth (about 1½ minutes total).

2. Place pretzel sticks in a large bowl; add white chocolate mixture, tossing gently to coat. Drop by rounded tablespoonfuls onto parchment paper. Place a candy pumpkin against side of each haystack. Cool completely.

Spooky Snack Mix

Makes 13 cups

6   (1-ounce) boxes candied popcorn and peanut mix
1   (12-ounce) bag candy corn
1   (14-ounce) bag orange and brown candy-coated chocolate pieces
1   (14-ounce) bag orange and brown candy-coated chocolate-covered peanuts
1   (10-ounce) box bear-shaped chocolate graham snacks
1   (8-ounce) bag bite-size cream-filled chocolate sandwich cookies

1. In a large bowl, combine candied popcorn mix, candies, graham snacks, and sandwich cookies. Toss gently to combine. Store snack mix in an airtight container.

Creepy Crawler Cupcakes

Makes 1 dozen

¾ cup sugar
⅓ cup butter, softened
2 large eggs, beaten
2 (1-ounce) squares unsweetened baking chocolate, melted and cooled
½ cup sour cream
¼ cup milk
1 teaspoon vanilla extract
¾ cup all-purpose flour
¼ cup unsweetened cocoa powder
½ teaspoon baking powder
¼ teaspoon baking soda
¼ teaspoon salt
Chocolate-Sour Cream Frosting (recipe follows)
Decoration: crushed chocolate sandwich cookies, worm-shaped chewy fruit snacks

1. Preheat oven to 350°. Line a 12-cup muffin pan with paper liners; set aside.

2. In a large bowl, combine sugar and butter. Beat at medium speed with an electric mixer until fluffy. Add eggs and chocolate; beat until creamy. Add sour cream, milk, and vanilla, beating until well combined.

3. In a separate bowl, sift together flour, cocoa, baking powder, baking soda, and salt. Reduce mixer speed to low; gradually add flour mixture to butter mixture. Beat until well combined (batter will be thick). Spoon batter into prepared muffin cups, filling each three-fourths full. Bake for 18 to 20 minutes or until a wooden pick inserted in center comes out clean. Cool in pan for 5 minutes; remove from pan, and cool completely on wire racks. Frost tops of cupcakes with Chocolate-Sour Cream Frosting. Decorate with crushed cookies and worm-shaped chewy fruit snacks.

CHOCOLATE-SOUR CREAM FROSTING

Makes 2 cups

¾ cup semisweet chocolate morsels
2 tablespoons butter
½ cup sour cream
½ teaspoon vanilla extract
1½ cups confectioners' sugar

1. In a medium microwave-safe bowl, microwave chocolate morsels and butter on High in 30-second intervals, stirring after each, until melted and smooth (about 1 minute total). Let chocolate mixture cool slightly.

2. Add sour cream and vanilla to cooled chocolate mixture. Beat at medium speed with an electric mixer until smooth and creamy.

3. Gradually add confectioners' sugar, beating until combined.

SEASON
& Spice

Spice up a wintertime holiday soiree with sophisticated style and bold tastes from the great state of Texas.

Menu

TOMATILLO PICO DE GALLO

CHEESY CHICKEN
STUFFED POBLANOS

BEEF BRISKET

CORN AND PEPPERS

SAVORY TEXAS BEANS

FLOURLESS CHOCOLATE-
CHIPOTLE CAKE WITH
CHOCOLATE GANACHE

Beef Brisket
Makes 10 to 12 servings

½ cup firmly packed light brown
    sugar
¼ cup smoked paprika
¼ cup hot chili powder
3 tablespoons ground coriander
2 tablespoons garlic powder
2 tablespoons onion powder
1 tablespoon ground black pepper
2 teaspoons salt
1 teaspoon ground red pepper
1 (8-pound) beef brisket
¼ cup olive oil

1. Preheat oven to 275°. In a medium bowl, combine brown sugar, paprika, chili powder, coriander, garlic powder, onion powder, pepper, salt, and red pepper.

2. Trim fat cap on brisket to ⅛-inch thickness. Rub entire surface of brisket with olive oil, and coat with brown sugar mixture. Place brisket, fat side up, in a large disposable aluminum roasting pan. Cover with aluminum foil. Bake for 6 hours.

Corn and Peppers
Makes 10 to 12 servings

½ cup butter
¾ cup chopped green onion
1 tablespoon minced garlic
6 cups fresh corn kernels
1 cup chopped poblano pepper
1 cup chopped red bell pepper
1 jalapeño pepper, seeded and
    minced
¼ cup chopped fresh cilantro
3 tablespoons fresh lime juice
1 teaspoon salt
¼ teaspoon ground red pepper
Garnish: fresh parsley

1. In a large nonstick skillet, melt butter over medium heat. Add green onion and garlic. Cook for 2 minutes, stirring constantly.

2. Add corn, poblano pepper, bell pepper, jalapeño, cilantro, lime juice, salt, and ground red pepper to onion mixture. Cook, stirring frequently, for 10 minutes or until tender. Garnish with parsley, if desired.

Red-hot holidays start with delicious dishes, and though that order may seem as tall as a 10-gallon hat, this Tex-Mex menu is big enough on flavor to fill it completely. This hearty meal would be welcome on the dinner table any time of year, but it is particularly palatable during the holidays and serves as a nice break from more traditional December fare.

Tomatillo Pico de Gallo
Makes about 3 cups

2	cups chopped tomatillo
2	cups seeded chopped tomato
½	cup finely chopped yellow onion
2	jalapeño peppers, seeded and minced
2	tablespoons fresh lime juice
2	tablespoons chopped fresh cilantro
2	teaspoons minced garlic
¾	teaspoon salt
½	teaspoon ground black pepper

1. In a medium bowl, combine tomatillo, tomato, onion, jalapeño, lime juice, cilantro, garlic, salt, and pepper. Cover and refrigerate for 2 hours. Serve with tortilla chips.

67

Savory Texas Beans

Makes 12 servings

2	tablespoons bacon drippings
1	large yellow onion, chopped
1	tablespoon minced garlic
2	(16-ounce) cans dark red kidney beans, drained
2	(16-ounce) cans pinto beans, drained
2	(15-ounce) cans black beans, drained
2½	cups chicken broth
2	(4-ounce) cans chopped green chiles
4	bay leaves
1	teaspoon ground cumin
½	teaspoon salt
½	teaspoon ground black pepper

1. In a large Dutch oven, heat bacon drippings over medium heat. Add onion; cook for 4 to 5 minutes or until tender. Add garlic; cook for 2 minutes, stirring frequently. Add beans, broth, chiles, bay leaves, cumin, salt, and pepper. Bring to a simmer. Reduce heat to low. Simmer, uncovered, for 1 hour, stirring occasionally. Remove and discard bay leaves.

Cheesy Chicken Stuffed Poblanos

Makes 12 servings

¼	cup butter
3	large yellow onions, sliced ⅛ inch thick
2	tablespoons balsamic vinegar
¾	teaspoon salt
½	teaspoon ground black pepper
12	large poblano peppers
6	cups chopped cooked chicken
4	cups shredded Colby Jack cheese
1½	cups grated Cotija cheese (Mexican Parmesan)
2	(14.5-ounce) cans diced fire-roasted tomatoes, well drained
1	(19-ounce) can enchilada sauce
2	tablespoons ancho chile powder

Garnish: grated Cotija cheese

1. In a Dutch oven, melt butter over medium-low heat. Add onions; cover and cook for 30 minutes, stirring occasionally.

2. Uncover onions, and increase heat to medium-high. Cook, stirring frequently, for 18 to 20 minutes or until golden brown. Add vinegar, salt, and pepper. Cook, stirring constantly, for 1 to 2 minutes or until liquid evaporates; set aside.

3. Preheat oven to 350°. Line a rimmed baking sheet with aluminum foil.

4. Cut a lengthwise slit down center of each pepper. Cut a 2-inch crosswise slit across top of each pepper to form a T. Carefully remove seeds from inside of peppers, leaving peppers intact.

5. In a large bowl, combine chicken, onion mixture, cheeses, tomatoes, enchilada sauce, and chile powder, stirring until well combined. Spoon about 1 cup filling into each pepper. Place on prepared baking sheet. Bake for 1 hour or until peppers are tender. Garnish with additional Cotija cheese, if desired.

Flourless Chocolate-Chipotle Cake

Makes 1 (9-inch) cake

1   cup semisweet chocolate morsels
¾   cup plus 2 tablespoons unsalted
     butter
5   large eggs, separated
2   teaspoons vanilla extract
¾   cup sugar
2   tablespoons unsweetened cocoa
     powder
1   teaspoon ground chipotle chile
     pepper
¼   teaspoon salt
Chocolate Ganache (recipe follows)
Garnish: red and green chile peppers

1. Preheat oven to 325°. Fill a roasting pan with 1 inch of hot water, and place in oven. Spray a 9-inch round cake pan with nonstick baking spray with flour. Line bottom with parchment paper; set aside.

2. In a small microwave-safe bowl, microwave chocolate morsels and butter on High in 30-second intervals, stirring after each, until melted and smooth (about 1 minute total). Cool chocolate mixture slightly.

3. In a medium bowl, whisk together egg yolks and vanilla. Add chocolate mixture, whisking until smooth.

4. In a separate bowl, combine sugar, cocoa powder, ground chipotle chile pepper, and salt. Add sugar mixture to chocolate mixture, stirring until well combined.

5. In a separate bowl, beat egg whites at medium speed with an electric mixer until soft peaks form. Fold egg whites, one-third at a time, into chocolate mixture. Spoon batter into prepared 9-inch pan. Place in oven in center of roasting pan.

6. Bake for 50 to 55 minutes or until a wooden pick inserted in center comes out clean.

7. Remove cake pan from hot water; cool cake in pan on a wire rack for 10 minutes. Remove from pan; cool completely on wire rack. Pour Chocolate Ganache over center of cake, allowing excess to cover sides. Garnish with chile peppers, if desired.

CHOCOLATE GANACHE
Makes 1⅓ cups

⅔   cup heavy whipping cream
2   tablespoons sugar
2   tablespoons light corn syrup
¾   cup semisweet chocolate morsels

1. In a small saucepan over medium heat, bring cream, sugar, and corn syrup to a boil. Add chocolate morsels, stirring until melted and smooth. Let cool slightly before using.

SEASIDE
Serenity

Drift away on a blissful breeze to an ocean paradise where a divine alfresco meal awaits. As you dine, bask in the summer sun and soak up the coastal views.

Menu

CUCUMBER SALAD WITH
TOMATO-BASIL VINAIGRETTE

FRIED GREEN TOMATO
CRAB CAKES WITH
GREEN ONION RÉMOULADE

SHRIMP AND LOBSTER LINGUINI

KEY LIME-RASPBERRY
CHEESECAKE

WHITE SANGRIA

Cucumber Salad with Tomato-Basil Vinaigrette
Makes 6 servings

1 seedless cucumber, thinly sliced
1 pint cherry tomatoes, halved
3 yellow squash, cut lengthwise and thinly sliced
1 small red onion, thinly sliced
Tomato-Basil Vinaigrette (recipe follows)

1. In a large bowl, combine cucumber, tomatoes, squash, and onion. Serve with Tomato-Basil Vinaigrette.

TOMATO-BASIL VINAIGRETTE
Makes 2 cups

½ cup red wine vinegar
⅓ cup firmly packed light brown sugar
¼ cup chopped fresh basil
¼ cup tomato paste
2 teaspoons Worcestershire sauce
1 teaspoon minced garlic
½ teaspoon dried oregano
¼ teaspoon salt
1 cup extra-virgin olive oil

1. In the work bowl of a food processor, combine vinegar, sugar, basil, tomato paste, Worcestershire sauce, garlic, oregano, and salt; process until blended. With food processor running, add oil in a slow, steady stream; process until blended. Cover and chill.

White Sangria
Makes about 3 quarts

2 (750-milliliter) bottles Riesling
1 (12-ounce) can frozen lemonade concentrate, thawed
2 cups pineapple juice
1½ cups pear-flavored vodka
½ cup sugar
2 kiwifruit, sliced
1 green Anjou pear, sliced
½ fresh pineapple, sliced
Garnish: fresh mint sprigs

1. In a large pitcher, combine wine, lemonade concentrate, pineapple juice, vodka, and sugar. Stir until sugar dissolves. Add fresh fruit; chill for 2 hours. Serve chilled or over ice. Garnish with fresh mint sprigs, if desired.

Fried Green Tomato Crab Cakes

Makes 6 to 8 servings

1   (8-ounce) container jumbo lump
    crabmeat, picked free of shell
1½ cups panko (Japanese
    breadcrumbs), divided
2   tablespoons minced red bell pepper
1   tablespoon minced green onion
1   tablespoon chopped fresh parsley
2   teaspoons Old Bay seasoning,
    divided
¾   teaspoon salt, divided
2   large eggs, divided
2   tablespoons mayonnaise
1   tablespoon fresh lemon juice
1   cup all-purpose flour
3   small green tomatoes, peeled
    and sliced ¼ inch thick
    (9 slices total)
1   cup olive oil
Green Onion Rémoulade
    (recipe follows)
Garnish: chopped fresh parsley,
    hot chili oil

1. In a medium bowl, combine crabmeat, ½ cup panko, bell pepper, green onion, parsley, 1 teaspoon Old Bay seasoning, and ¼ teaspoon salt. In a small bowl, lightly beat 1 egg; whisk in mayonnaise and lemon juice. Add egg mixture to crab mixture, tossing to combine.

2. In a shallow dish, combine remaining 1 cup panko and remaining 1 teaspoon Old Bay seasoning. Set aside.

3. In a separate shallow dish, combine flour and remaining ½ teaspoon salt. Coat tomato slices in flour mixture. Shape about 2 tablespoons crab mixture on top of each tomato slice.

4. In a small bowl, lightly beat remaining egg. Lightly brush both sides of crab cakes with egg, and coat with panko mixture.

5. In a large nonstick skillet, heat oil over medium heat. Add crab cakes, and cook for 3 to 4 minutes per side or until golden brown. Drain on paper towels. Serve with Green Onion Rémoulade. Garnish with parsley and chili oil, if desired.

GREEN ONION RÉMOULADE
Makes about 2 cups

1   cup mayonnaise
1   bunch green onions, green
    parts only
2   tablespoons Creole mustard
2   tablespoons sour cream
¼   cup sweet pickle relish
2   tablespoons chopped fresh
    parsley
1   tablespoon capers, rinsed and
    drained
1   teaspoon minced garlic
¼   teaspoon ground black pepper
Garnish: chopped green onion

1. In the work bowl of a food processor, combine mayonnaise, green onion tops, mustard, and sour cream; process until well blended. Add relish, parsley, capers, garlic, and pepper; pulse until combined. Cover and chill. Garnish with chopped green onion, if desired.

Shrimp and Lobster Linguini

Makes 6 to 8 servings

3   tablespoons butter
2   tablespoons minced garlic
⅔   cup dry white wine
3   tablespoons fresh lemon juice
3   cups heavy whipping cream
½   teaspoon salt
¼   teaspoon ground black pepper
¼   teaspoon ground red pepper
2   pounds large fresh shrimp, peeled
    and deveined (tails left on)
2   (10-ounce) lobster tails, cooked
    and chopped (about 2 cups
    chopped, cooked lobster meat)
6   cups fresh baby spinach leaves
1   (1-pound) box linguini, cooked
    and kept warm

1. In a large Dutch oven, melt butter over medium heat. Add garlic, and cook for 2 minutes, stirring constantly. Add wine and lemon juice, and cook for 4 minutes.

2. Add cream, salt, black pepper, and red pepper; cook for 15 to 20 minutes or until thickened slightly.

3. Add shrimp, and cook for 3 to 4 minutes or until shrimp are pink. Add lobster and spinach, and cook for 1 to 2 minutes or until spinach wilts. Serve over hot cooked linguini.

Key Lime-Raspberry Cheesecake

Makes 1 (9½-inch) cheesecake

Crust:
- 2 cups firmly packed vanilla wafer crumbs
- ⅓ cup sugar
- 6 tablespoons butter, melted

Filling:
- 4 (8-ounce) packages cream cheese, softened
- 1½ cups sugar
- 5 large eggs
- ½ cup Key lime juice
- 1 tablespoon lime zest
- 2 tablespoons all-purpose flour
- 1 (8-ounce) container sour cream
- 1½ cups fresh raspberries
- Garnish: Key lime slices, raspberries, raspberry syrup, lime zest

1. To prepare crust: Preheat oven to 300°. In a small bowl, combine vanilla wafer crumbs, sugar, and melted butter. Press firmly on bottom and up sides of a 9½-inch springform pan. Bake for 10 minutes; set aside to cool.

2. To prepare filling: In a large bowl, beat cream cheese and sugar at medium speed with an electric mixer until fluffy. Add eggs, one at a time, beating well after each addition. Add Key lime juice, lime zest, and flour, beating just until combined. Stir in sour cream.

3. Arrange raspberries evenly in bottom of prepared crust. Cover raspberries with cheesecake batter. Bake for 1 hour and 15 minutes; turn oven off. Let cheesecake stand in oven with door closed for 4 hours.

4. Remove cheesecake from oven. Gently run a knife around edge of pan to release sides. Cool completely in pan on a wire rack. Cover and chill for 8 hours. Remove sides of pan to serve. Garnish with Key lime slices, raspberries, raspberry syrup, and lime zest, if desired.

SPLENDOR
in the Grass

Stop. Slow down. Take a look around. Beauty is everywhere—in the vibrant colors of fresh flowers, the lush carpet of green grass, the wild freedom of the great outdoors.

Menu

ARTICHOKE HUMMUS WITH TOASTED PITA CHIPS

MEDITERRANEAN CHICKEN WRAPS WITH CREAMY FETA DRESSING

LEMON-ALMOND COOKIES

Packed with flavor, this picnic is sure to please the palate. The menu combines fabulous tastes from the Mediterranean with the ease and artful presentation that we Southerners love. Serve chilled white wine and fresh fruit to round out the fare for this portable feast.

Artichoke Hummus with Toasted Pita Chips
Makes about 3 cups

1   (16-ounce) can chickpeas, drained
1   (14-ounce) can small artichoke hearts, drained
½   cup tahini paste
6   tablespoons olive oil
3   tablespoons fresh lemon juice
2   tablespoons chopped fresh parsley
1   teaspoon minced garlic
1   teaspoon salt
1   teaspoon paprika
¼   teaspoon ground red pepper
⅛   teaspoon ground white pepper
Toasted Pita Chips (recipe follows)

1. In the work bowl of a food processor, combine first 11 ingredients; process until smooth. Serve with Toasted Pita Chips.

TOASTED PITA CHIPS
Makes 4 servings

4   pita bread rounds, cut into triangles
2   tablespoons olive oil
½   teaspoon garlic salt

1. Preheat oven to 400°. Brush both sides of pita triangles with olive oil. Place on an ungreased baking sheet. Sprinkle tops with garlic salt. Bake for 8 minutes or until golden brown. Cool completely; store in an airtight container.

Mediterranean Chicken Wraps
Makes 4 servings

4   (8-inch) sun-dried tomato-flavored tortillas
1   head green leaf lettuce, shredded
2   cups precooked grilled chicken pieces or sliced cooked chicken
½   cup sliced black olives
2   medium tomatoes, seeded and chopped
1   yellow bell pepper, cut into ¼-inch-thick strips
Creamy Feta Dressing (recipe follows)

1. Layer each tortilla with lettuce, chicken, black olives, tomato, and bell pepper, leaving a ½-inch border around edges of tortillas. Roll up, and secure with wooden picks. Serve immediately, or wrap each sandwich in heavy-duty plastic wrap, and chill. Serve with Creamy Feta Dressing.

CREAMY FETA DRESSING
Makes about 1½ cups

½   cup sour cream
½   cup mayonnaise
1   (5-ounce) container crumbled feta cheese
2   teaspoons fresh lemon juice
1   teaspoon Dijon mustard
¼   teaspoon sugar
¼   teaspoon salt
¼   teaspoon ground black pepper

1. In the work bowl of a food processor, combine all ingredients; process until well combined. Cover and chill.

Lemon-Almond Cookies

Makes 2 dozen

½   cup unsalted butter, softened
¾   cup sugar
2   tablespoons frozen lemonade
     concentrate, thawed
2   teaspoons lemon zest
¼   teaspoon almond extract
1½   cups self-rising flour
Sugar
Sliced almonds

1. Preheat oven to 325°. Line a baking sheet with parchment paper.

2. In a medium bowl, beat butter and sugar at medium speed with an electric mixer until fluffy. Add lemonade concentrate, lemon zest, and almond extract, beating until combined. Gradually add flour, beating just until combined.

3. Roll dough into 1-inch balls; place on prepared baking sheet. Using the bottom of a glass dipped in additional sugar, flatten each ball to a 2-inch round. Press sliced almonds firmly into each cookie. Bake for 14 to 16 minutes or until lightly browned. Cool on pan for 2 minutes; remove to wire racks, and cool completely. Store in an airtight container.

83

Sizzlin' SUPPER

Warm summer nights. Cool peachy drinks. It doesn't get much better than this—that is, until you fire up the grill and gather your friends for a relaxed dinner party with a spicy spread.

Menu

CREAMY GUACAMOLE

SUMMER SALSA

MARINATED FLANK STEAK

ROASTED CORN AND POBLANO SALAD

SAVORY BLACK BEANS

BANANA CHIMICHANGAS

PEACH MARGARITAS

Whether we're toasting a big birthday, celebrating Cinco de Mayo, or just enjoying another joyful Saturday night in June, Southerners rarely need an excuse for alfresco entertaining. So call up your closest companions, select a patio or porch, and fill the space with twinkling lights. A simple setting combined with plenty of plants creates an island-like atmosphere where you and your company can truly kick back and relax.

Creamy Guacamole
Makes about 5 cups

8 ripe avocados, mashed
1 large tomato, seeded and chopped
6 tablespoons chopped fresh cilantro
¼ cup finely chopped red onion
¼ cup sour cream
3 tablespoons fresh lime juice
2 teaspoons garlic salt

1. Place all ingredients in a medium bowl, stirring until well combined. Cover and chill.

Summer Salsa
Makes about 5½ cups

1 (28-ounce) can crushed tomatoes
1 (10-ounce) can diced tomatoes with green chiles
3 cloves garlic, minced
2 jalapeño peppers, seeded and minced
3 tablespoons fresh lime juice
2 tablespoons fresh lemon juice
1 teaspoon salt
½ teaspoon ground black pepper
1 large onion, chopped
1 bunch fresh cilantro, chopped

1. In the work bowl of a food processor, combine crushed tomatoes, diced tomatoes, garlic, jalapeño, lime juice, lemon juice, salt, and pepper. Pulse until desired consistency is reached.

2. Add onion and cilantro, and pulse until desired consistency is reached. Cover and chill for 2 hours. Store in refrigerator in an airtight container up to 3 days.

Savory Black Beans
Makes 6 servings

2 tablespoons bacon drippings
1 medium-size yellow onion, chopped
1 teaspoon minced garlic
3 (15-ounce) cans black beans, drained
1 (14-ounce) can chicken broth
1 (4.5-ounce) can chopped green chiles
2 bay leaves
½ teaspoon ground cumin
½ teaspoon salt
½ teaspoon ground black pepper

1. In a large Dutch oven, heat bacon drippings over medium heat. Add onion; cook for 2 to 3 minutes or until lightly browned. Add garlic; cook for 1 minute. Add beans, broth, chiles, bay leaves, cumin, salt, and pepper. Bring to a simmer. Reduce heat to low; simmer, uncovered, for 1 hour, stirring occasionally. Remove and discard bay leaves.

Peach Margaritas
Makes 6 servings

1 (20-ounce) bag frozen sliced peaches
1 (11.3-ounce) can peach nectar
¾ cup tequila
¼ cup peach schnapps
¼ cup sugar
2 tablespoons fresh lemon juice
Garnish: sugar, fresh peach slices

1. In the container of a blender, combine peaches and nectar. Process until smooth. Add tequila, schnapps, sugar, and lemon juice. Process until smooth.

2. Moisten glass rims, and dip in sugar to coat, if desired. Fill glasses with peach mixture. Garnish with peach slices, if desired. Serve immediately.

Roasted Corn and Poblano Salad

Makes 4 to 6 servings

4   cups fresh corn kernels (about 8 ears)
2   poblano peppers, halved and seeded
1   red bell pepper, halved and seeded
3   tablespoons chopped green onion
¼   cup sour cream
2   tablespoons mayonnaise
1   tablespoon fresh lime juice
½   teaspoon minced chipotle pepper in adobo sauce
½   teaspoon salt
½   teaspoon chili powder
Garnish: chopped green onion

1. Preheat oven to 500°. Line a rimmed baking sheet with aluminum foil.

2. Place corn and peppers on prepared pan. Bake for 25 minutes or until corn and peppers appear blistered, stirring corn halfway through baking time.

3. Place peppers in a resealable plastic bag; seal and let stand for 10 minutes to loosen skins. Remove and discard pepper skins, and chop peppers. Cool corn and peppers completely.

4. In a medium bowl, combine corn, peppers, and green onion. In a separate bowl, combine sour cream, mayonnaise, lime juice, chipotle pepper, salt, and chili powder. Add sour cream mixture to corn mixture, tossing to coat. Garnish with green onion, if desired. Cover and chill.

Marinated Flank Steak

Makes 6 servings

1   red onion, chopped
1   bunch fresh cilantro, chopped
½   cup red wine vinegar
½   cup olive oil
¼   cup fresh lime juice
¼   cup fresh lemon juice
¼   cup firmly packed dark brown sugar
3   tablespoons lime zest
2   tablespoons minced garlic
1½   teaspoons salt
¼   teaspoon ground black pepper
1   (2-pound) flank steak or 2 (1-pound) flank steaks

1. Combine onion, cilantro, vinegar, oil, lime juice, lemon juce, brown sugar, zest, garlic, salt, and pepper in a shallow dish or a large resealable plastic bag; add steak. Cover or seal, and chill for 12 hours, turning steak occasionally.

2. Remove steak from marinade, discarding marinade. Cook steak, without grill lid, over medium-high heat (350° to 400°) for about 5 minutes on each side or until desired degree of doneness. Let steak rest for 5 minutes before slicing diagonally across grain.

Banana Chimichangas

Makes 6 servings

¼   cup butter
¾   cup firmly packed dark brown sugar
½   teaspoon ground cinnamon
3   tablespoons gold rum
4   bananas, sliced
6   (6-inch) flour tortillas
Vegetable oil for frying
2   tablespoons cinnamon sugar
Toppings: vanilla ice cream, caramel ice-cream topping, chopped pecans (optional)

1. In a medium sauté pan, melt butter over medium heat. Add brown sugar and cinnamon; cook for 3 to 4 minutes, stirring constantly. Carefully add rum, and cook for 2 minutes, stirring frequently. Add bananas, stirring gently to coat. Remove from heat; cool mixture slightly.

2. Spoon about 3 tablespoons banana mixture in center of each tortilla. Fold in sides, and roll up tortillas. Secure with wooden picks.

3. In a Dutch oven, pour oil to a depth of 2 inches; heat to 350°. Fry two filled tortillas at a time for 1 to 2 minutes or until golden brown. Drain on paper towels. Sprinkle with cinnamon sugar.

4. To serve, top warm chimichangas with vanilla ice cream, caramel topping, and chopped pecans, if desired.

SUMMER
Splash

Slip into something cool and casual, and join the party poolside. Refreshing sippers and savory appetizers await, so dive on in and enjoy the fun!

Menu

CUCUMBER CANAPÉS

SHRIMP BRUSCHETTA

MINI CHICKEN AND
CHIPOTLE QUESADILLAS

MARGARITA MOUSSE

STRAWBERRY MOJITO

BLUEBERRY COOLER

Blueberry Cooler

Makes about 1 gallon

9   cups water
3   cups fresh lime juice
2½   cups sugar
1   cup blueberry-flavored syrup
Garnish: lime slices, fresh blueberries

1. Combine water, lime juice, sugar, and syrup in a 1-gallon pitcher. Stir until sugar dissolves. Chill; serve over ice. Garnish with lime slices and blueberries, if desired.

Strawberry Mojito

Makes 1 drink

¼   cup fresh lime juice
3   ounces light rum
3   ounces Strawberry-Mint Simple Syrup (recipe follows)
2   ounces club soda
Fresh mint leaves
Sliced fresh strawberries
Garnish: fresh strawberries,
        fresh mint leaves

1. In a shaker or 2-cup liquid measuring cup, combine lime juice, rum, simple syrup, and club soda; stir gently to mix. Place mint leaves and strawberries in bottom of a highball glass. Fill glass with ice; pour drink over ice. Garnish with strawberries and mint leaves, if desired.

STRAWBERRY-MINT SIMPLE SYRUP

Makes about 1 quart

3   cups water
3   cups sugar
3   cups chopped fresh strawberries
½   cup fresh mint leaves

1. In a large saucepan, combine water and sugar over medium-high heat; stir until sugar dissolves. Add strawberries, and bring to a simmer. Reduce heat to medium, and cook for 15 minutes. Remove from heat, and add mint leaves. Cover and steep for 10 minutes. Strain syrup, and cool completely. Store in airtight container for up to 2 weeks.

Cucumber Canapés
Makes about 5 dozen

2   seedless cucumbers
1   (8-ounce) package cream cheese,
    softened
3   tablespoons finely chopped red
    bell pepper
3   tablespoons finely chopped green
    bell pepper
3   tablespoons finely chopped
    yellow bell pepper
2   tablespoons minced green onion
1   tablespoon chopped fresh dill
½   teaspoon dry mustard
½   teaspoon garlic salt
½   teaspoon hot pepper sauce
¼   teaspoon garlic powder
Garnish: chopped fresh dill

1. Score cucumbers with a channel knife, and cut into ¼-inch-thick slices. In a small bowl, combine cream cheese, bell pepper, onion, dill, mustard, salt, hot pepper sauce, and garlic powder. Spoon cream cheese mixture over cucumber slices. Garnish with dill, if desired.

Mini Chicken and Chipotle Quesadillas

Makes 3 dozen

3	tablespoons butter
2	large onions, sliced ⅛ inch thick
¾	teaspoon salt, divided
¼	teaspoon ground black pepper
2	ripe avocados, mashed
2	tablespoons chopped fresh cilantro
1	tablespoon fresh lime juice
½	teaspoon garlic salt
2	cups chopped cooked chicken
1	cup shredded Monterey Jack cheese
½	cup sour cream
2½	teaspoons minced chipotle pepper in adobo sauce
¼	teaspoon ground cumin
2	tablespoons olive oil
3	(10-inch) flour tortillas

Garnish: chopped fresh tomato, fresh cilantro leaves

1. In a medium sauté pan, melt butter over medium-low heat. Add onions; cover and cook for 30 minutes, stirring occasionally. Uncover and increase heat to medium-high. Cook, stirring frequently, for 5 to 6 minutes or until brown. Stir in ½ teaspoon salt and pepper; remove from heat, and cool.

2. In a small bowl, combine avocado, cilantro, juice, and garlic salt; set aside. In a medium bowl, combine onions, chicken, cheese, sour cream, chipotle pepper, cumin, and remaining ¼ teaspoon salt.

3. Preheat broiler. Brush 2 baking sheets with oil. With a 2¼-inch round cutter, cut 36 circles from tortillas; place on prepared baking sheets. Spoon about 1 tablespoon chicken filling on each tortilla round. Broil 6 inches from heat for 5 to 7 minutes or until browned and bubbly. Top with avocado mixture. Garnish with tomato and cilantro, if desired.

Shrimp Bruschetta

Makes 2½ dozen

2	cups seeded chopped tomato (about 3 large tomatoes)
4	tablespoons olive oil, divided
2	tablespoons chopped fresh basil
1	tablespoon fresh lemon juice
1	tablespoon balsamic vinegar
1	tablespoon chopped capers
2	teaspoons minced garlic
½	teaspoon salt
¼	teaspoon ground black pepper
30	fresh jumbo shrimp, peeled and deveined
2	teaspoons Italian seasoning
½	teaspoon garlic salt
30	toasted French bread rounds

1. In a medium bowl, combine tomato, 2 tablespoons olive oil, basil, lemon juice, balsamic vinegar, capers, garlic, salt, and pepper. Cover and set aside.

2. In a medium bowl, combine shrimp, Italian seasoning, and garlic salt; toss gently to coat shrimp.

3. In a large sauté pan, heat remaining 2 tablespoons olive oil over medium-high heat. Cook shrimp for 1 to 2 minutes on each side or just until pink. Spoon about 1 tablespoon tomato mixture on top of each toasted bread round. Place shrimp on top of tomato mixture.

Margarita Mousse

Makes 8 to 10 servings

5	egg yolks
1	cup sugar
1	tablespoon lemon zest
1	tablespoon lemon juice
1	tablespoon lime zest
1	tablespoon lime juice
½	cup margarita mix
⅛	teaspoon salt
4	tablespoons butter, cut into pieces
2	tablespoons tequila
1	drop green food coloring (optional)
1	cup heavy whipping cream

Garnish: lime slices

1. In a medium heavy-duty saucepan, whisk together egg yolks, sugar, lemon zest, lemon juice, lime zest, lime juice, margarita mix, and salt. Cook over medium heat, whisking constantly, for 7 to 8 minutes or until thickened. Remove from heat; whisk in butter, tequila, and food coloring, if desired. Cool for 20 minutes; cover and chill for 2 hours.

2. In a medium bowl, beat cream at high speed with an electric mixer until stiff peaks form. Fold whipped cream into margarita-custard mixture. Chill until ready to serve. Garnish with lime slices, if desired.

Note: Make mousse 1 day ahead to save time. To get our look, moisten rims of mini margarita glasses and dip in sugar.

Candlelight
PICNIC

Deep red roses and the flicker of flames invite valentines to dine in romantic style.

Menu

VALENTINE HEARTS SALAD WITH CREAMY BALSAMIC ITALIAN DRESSING

VEAL PICCATA

PASTA WITH MUSHROOMS AND ROASTED GARLIC

SWEETHEART TARTS

Veal Piccata

Makes 2 servings

½   cup all-purpose flour
½   teaspoon salt
¼   teaspoon ground black pepper
½   pound veal cutlets
4   tablespoons butter, divided
2   tablespoons olive oil
2   tablespoons capers
2   teaspoons minced garlic
½   cup chicken broth
¼   cup dry white wine
¼   cup fresh lemon juice
1   tablespoon chopped fresh parsley

1. Preheat oven to 200°. In a shallow dish, combine flour, salt, and pepper. Coat veal in flour mixture, shaking off excess.

2. In a large nonstick skillet, melt 2 tablespoons butter with oil over medium-high heat. Add veal; cook for 1½ to 2 minutes per side or until golden brown. Remove from heat. Transfer veal to a rimmed baking sheet; keep warm in oven.

3. Return skillet to stovetop over medium heat. Add capers and garlic; cook for 1 minute. Add chicken broth, wine, and lemon juice; cook for 4 minutes, stirring frequently. Add parsley and remaining 2 tablespoons butter. Cook, stirring constantly, until butter melts and sauce thickens slightly, about 1 minute. Remove from heat. To serve, place veal on plates, and top with desired amount of sauce.

Valentine Hearts Salad

Makes 2 servings

4   cups torn green leaf lettuce
1   cup small artichoke hearts, halved
2   hearts of palm, sliced
½   cup chopped prosciutto
Creamy Balsamic Italian Dressing (recipe follows)
Garnish: toasted pine nuts, shaved Parmigiano-Reggiano cheese

1. Divide lettuce, artichoke hearts, hearts of palm, and prosciutto evenly between two salad plates. Drizzle with Creamy Balsamic Italian Dressing just before serving. Garnish with toasted pine nuts and cheese, if desired.

CREAMY BALSAMIC ITALIAN DRESSING
Makes about 1 cup

¾   cup mayonnaise
¼   cup buttermilk
¼   cup balsamic vinegar
1   tablespoon Italian seasoning
½   teaspoon sugar
¼   teaspoon garlic salt
¼   teaspoon ground black pepper

1. In a small bowl, combine all ingredients, whisking until smooth. Cover and chill until ready to serve.

Pasta with Mushrooms and Roasted Garlic

Makes 2 servings

2   tablespoons butter
2   tablespoons olive oil
1   (8-ounce) container sliced baby
     bella mushrooms
½   cup chopped leek
¼   cup dry white wine
1   tablespoon chopped roasted
     garlic
3   cups cooked fettuccine noodles
2   tablespoons chopped fresh basil
½   teaspoon salt
½   teaspoon ground black pepper
Garnish: freshly grated Parmigiano-
     Reggiano cheese, fresh basil

1. In a large sauté pan, melt butter with olive oil over medium heat. Add mushrooms and leek; cook for 7 to 8 minutes. Add wine and roasted garlic; cook for 1 minute, stirring constantly. Add fettuccine, basil, salt, and pepper; toss gently to combine. Garnish with cheese and fresh basil, if desired.

Sweetheart Tarts

Makes 4 servings

½   (14.1-ounce) package refrigerated
     pie crusts
1   (3-ounce) package cream cheese,
     softened
2   tablespoons seedless raspberry
     preserves
2   tablespoons confectioners' sugar
1   tablespoon raspberry-flavored
     liqueur
½   cup semisweet chocolate morsels
2   tablespoons heavy whipping
     cream
1   teaspoon light corn syrup,
     divided
Garnish: fresh raspberries,
     chocolate curls

1. Preheat oven to 450°. Spray 4 (3½-inch) heart-shaped tart pans with nonstick cooking spray; set aside.

2. On a lightly floured surface, unroll crust. Using a 4½-inch round cutter, cut 4 circles from crust. Line prepared pans with crusts; crimp edges, if desired. Prick bottoms of crusts with a fork. Place on a baking sheet; bake for 10 to 12 minutes or until golden brown. Cool in pans for 2 minutes. Remove from pans, and cool completely on a wire rack.

3. In a small bowl, combine cream cheese, raspberry preserves, confectioners' sugar, and liqueur. Beat at medium speed with an electric mixer until smooth; set aside.

4. In a small microwave-safe bowl, combine chocolate morsels, cream, and corn syrup. Microwave on High in 30-second intervals, stirring after each, until chocolate is melted and smooth (about 1 minute total).

5. Spread cream cheese mixture in bottoms of tart shells. Spread chocolate mixture over cream cheese mixture. Garnish with raspberries and chocolate curls, if desired.

AUTUMN
Allure

Take advantage of blue skies and beautiful weather to spend the day outside celebrating the bounteous gifts of the harvest.

Menu

GARLIC AND PARSLEY FOCACCIA

APPLE-PECAN STUFFED PORK LOIN

ROASTED FALL VEGETABLES

SWISS CHARD WITH PEPPERS

CARAMEL-APPLE TART

APPLE-LEMON TEA

There's a whisper of fall in the breeze that blows across the field, stirring the blades of grass in waves of jubilation. Neighboring trees happily observe this vibrant scene as they anxiously await their turn to join in the festivities by shedding their summer green and donning cloaks of orange, red, and yellow.

The vista spreads out like a watercolor painting: rolling farmland as far as the eye can see, bundles of sweet hay bleaching in the sun, cattle peacefully grazing in the distance, and, above it all, a canopy of brilliant blue.

Apple-Lemon Tea
Makes 1 gallon

6   cups water
3   family-size tea bags
½   cup sugar
1   (64-ounce) bottle apple cider
1   (12-ounce) can frozen lemonade
    concentrate, thawed

1. In a large Dutch oven, bring water to a boil over high heat. Remove from heat, and add tea bags. Cover and steep for 5 minutes. Remove and discard tea bags. Add sugar, stirring until sugar dissolves. Add apple cider and lemonade concentrate, stirring until well combined. Serve chilled or over ice.

Garlic and Parsley Focaccia
Makes 6 to 8 servings

1¼   cups warm water (105° to 115°)
2   teaspoons sugar
1   (¼-ounce) envelope active dry
     yeast
3¾   cups all-purpose flour
1½   teaspoons salt
3   tablespoons olive oil, divided
1   tablespoon minced garlic
1½   teaspoons chopped fresh parsley
¼   teaspoon kosher salt

1. Combine water, sugar, and yeast in a 2-cup liquid measuring cup; let stand for 5 minutes or until foamy.

2. In the work bowl of a food processor, combine flour and salt. Pulse several times to combine. With processor running, slowly add yeast mixture and 1 tablespoon olive oil. Continue running processor until mixture forms a ball.

3. On a lightly floured surface, turn out dough, and knead for 5 minutes. Place in a bowl coated with nonstick cooking spray, turning to coat top. Cover and let rise in a warm place (85°), free from drafts, for 1 hour or until dough is doubled in size.

4. Preheat oven to 400°. Grease a baking sheet with 1 tablespoon olive oil.

5. Punch down dough; knead lightly 4 or 5 times. Press dough into an 8½-x10½-inch rectangle; place on prepared baking sheet. Press handle of a wooden spoon into dough to make indentations at 1-inch intervals. Brush with remaining olive oil. Sprinkle with garlic, parsley, and salt, pressing lightly to adhere. Bake for 15 to 20 minutes or until lightly browned.

Swiss Chard with Peppers
Makes 6 servings

2   tablespoons butter
2   tablespoons olive oil
2   yellow bell peppers, cut into
     ⅛-inch-wide strips
2   red bell peppers, cut into
     ⅛-inch-wide strips
2   teaspoons minced garlic
3   pounds Swiss chard, stems
     removed and chopped
     (about 3 bunches)
2   tablespoons apple cider vinegar
2   tablespoons chicken broth
1   teaspoon salt
½   teaspoon ground black pepper

1. In a large Dutch oven, melt butter with olive oil over medium-high heat. Add bell peppers, and cook for 5 to 6 minutes or until crisp-tender. Add garlic, and cook for 2 minutes. Add Swiss chard, tossing to coat with oil; cook until wilted. Stir in vinegar, broth, salt, and pepper.

Apple-Pecan Stuffed Pork Loin

Makes 6 to 8 servings

4	slices applewood smoked bacon
1½	cups chopped Gala apple
¾	cup chopped celery
¾	cup chopped onion
3	cloves garlic, minced
1	teaspoon sugar
1½	teaspoons salt, divided
¾	teaspoon ground black pepper, divided
1	cup crumbled cornbread
½	cup toasted chopped pecans
2	tablespoons chopped fresh thyme
¼	cup chicken broth
1	(4-pound) boneless pork loin, trimmed
2	tablespoons olive oil
	Apple Cider Glaze (recipe follows)

1. In a large skillet, cook bacon over medium heat for 6 to 7 minutes or until crisp. Remove bacon to paper towels to drain, reserving drippings in skillet. Crumble bacon.

2. Add apple, celery, onion, garlic, sugar, ½ teaspoon salt, and ¼ teaspoon pepper to drippings. Cook for 5 to 6 minutes or until tender; remove from heat. Add cornbread, pecans, thyme, broth, and bacon, stirring until well combined.

3. Preheat oven to 475°.

4. Place pork loin on a clean surface. Cut into one long side of loin, leaving a ½-inch border; continue cutting in a circular pattern until loin can be rolled out into a rectangle that is about ½-inch thick. Top with heavy-duty plastic wrap. Using a meat mallet, pound pork to an even ½-inch thickness.

5. Spread cornbread mixture over pork, leaving a 1-inch border. Starting at a long side, roll up pork, jelly-roll style. Secure at 2-inch intervals with butcher's twine. Rub outside of pork with oil; sprinkle with remaining 1 teaspoon salt and ½ teaspoon pepper. Place, seam side down, in a roasting pan. Bake for 20 minutes.

6. Reduce oven temperature to 325°. Pour Apple Cider Glaze over pork, and loosely cover with aluminum foil. Bake for 30 to 40 minutes or until a meat thermometer inserted in center registers 150°, basting periodically. Let rest for 10 minutes. Spoon glaze from pan over pork loin.

APPLE CIDER GLAZE

Makes 1½ cups

1	tablespoon butter
1	tablespoon olive oil
2	tablespoons chopped fresh thyme
2	teaspoons minced garlic
1	cup apple cider
2	tablespoons apple cider vinegar
¼	cup soy sauce
½	cup firmly packed light brown sugar
½	teaspoon salt
¼	teaspoon ground black pepper

1. In a medium saucepan, melt butter with oil over medium heat. Add thyme and garlic; cook for 1 to 2 minutes. Add remaining ingredients. Bring to a simmer. Cook for 5 minutes, stirring frequently.

Roasted Fall Vegetables

Makes 6 to 8 servings

4	carrots, peeled and sliced into ½-inch pieces
4	parsnips, peeled and sliced into ½-inch pieces
1	sweet potato, peeled and diced into ½-inch cubes
1	butternut squash, peeled and diced into ½-inch cubes
1	(10-ounce) bag red or white pearl onions, peeled
6	tablespoons olive oil
2	tablespoons chopped fresh rosemary
1¾	teaspoons salt
½	teaspoon ground black pepper

1. Preheat oven to 450°. Line a rimmed baking sheet with aluminum foil. In a large bowl, combine all vegetables.

2. In a small bowl, combine oil, rosemary, salt, and pepper; pour over vegetables, tossing to coat. Arrange vegetables in an even layer on pan. Bake for 20 minutes or until tender, stirring once halfway through. Broil for 4 to 5 minutes.

Caramel-
Apple Tart
Makes 1 (9-inch) tart

½ (14.1-ounce) package refrigerated pie crust
2 Granny Smith apples, cut into ⅛-inch-thick slices
2 Gala apples, cut into ⅛-inch-thick slices
¼ cup honey, warmed
2 tablespoons fresh lemon juice
¾ cup sugar
¼ cup cornstarch
½ teaspoon ground cinnamon
½ teaspoon ground cardamom
⅛ teaspoon salt
Melted caramel
Garnish: chopped pecans

1. Preheat oven to 400°. Fit pie crust into a 9-inch tart pan with removable bottom.

2. In a medium bowl, combine apples, honey, and lemon juice.

3. In a small bowl, combine sugar, cornstarch, cinnamon, cardamom, and salt. Add sugar mixture to apple mixture; toss gently to coat.

4. Arrange apple slices in concentric circles in prepared crust; pour any sugar mixture remaining in bowl over apples. Bake for 30 to 35 minutes or until lightly browned. Cool in pan for 10 minutes; remove from pan, and cool completely. Drizzle with melted caramel. Garnish with chopped pecans, if desired.

FALL
Outdoors

Follow the forest path to a clearing down by the creek bank where an enchanted table awaits. Laden with harvest delights, it beckons you to take a seat for a truly unforgettable evening.

Menu

WHITE PUMPKIN SOUP WITH SPICY TOASTED PUMPKIN SEEDS

WALNUT-CRUSTED CHICKEN WITH CREAMY PUMPKIN SAUCE

BALSAMIC-GLAZED BRUSSELS SPROUTS

SAUTÉED PEARS AND APPLES

PUMPKIN-PIE ICE CREAM WITH PECAN CRUMBLE TOPPING

White Pumpkin Soup

Makes 6 to 8 servings

2	tablespoons butter
2	tablespoons olive oil
1	cup chopped onion
1	cup chopped carrot
1	cup chopped parsnip
1	tablespoon minced garlic
2	tablespoons all-purpose flour
6	cups chicken broth
3	cups white pumpkin puree
1½	teaspoons ground cumin
1	teaspoon salt
¼	teaspoon ground black pepper
2	cups heavy whipping cream
½	cup sour cream

Spicy Toasted Pumpkin Seeds
(recipe follows)

1. In a medium Dutch oven, melt butter with olive oil over medium heat. Add onion, carrot, parsnip, and garlic. Cook, stirring frequently, for 12 minutes or until tender. Add flour; cook, stirring constantly, for 1 minute. Add chicken broth, pumpkin puree, cumin, salt, and pepper. Reduce heat to low; cook for 10 minutes.

2. In the work bowl of a food processor, puree pumpkin mixture, in batches if necessary, until smooth. Return pureed mixture to Dutch oven. Add cream and sour cream, whisking until smooth. Bring to a simmer over medium heat, and simmer for 2 minutes or until heated through. Top servings with Spicy Toasted Pumpkin Seeds.

SPICY TOASTED PUMPKIN SEEDS

Makes 2 cups

3	tablespoons butter, melted
1	teaspoon garlic powder
½	teaspoon ancho chile powder
½	teaspoon ground cumin
½	teaspoon seasoned salt
¼	teaspoon ground red pepper
2	cups pumpkin seeds

1. Preheat oven to 350°. Line a rimmed baking sheet with aluminum foil.

2. In a small bowl, combine butter, garlic powder, chile powder, cumin, seasoned salt, and red pepper. Add pumpkin seeds, tossing gently to coat. Spread pumpkin seeds in an even layer on prepared pan. Bake for 20 to 25 minutes or until lightly browned; cool completely. Store in an airtight container.

Balsamic-Glazed Brussels Sprouts

Makes 6 servings

4	slices thick-sliced bacon
1	tablespoon minced garlic
½	cup balsamic vinegar
1½	tablespoons sugar
¾	teaspoon salt
½	teaspoon ground black pepper
2	pounds fresh Brussels sprouts, halved

1. In a large nonstick skillet, cook bacon over medium heat for 15 minutes or until crisp. Remove bacon to paper towels to drain, reserving ¼ cup drippings in skillet. Crumble bacon; set aside. Add garlic to reserved drippings in skillet; cook over medium heat for 1 minute. Stir in vinegar, sugar, salt, and pepper. Add Brussels sprouts, stirring to coat; cover and cook for 5 minutes. Uncover, increase heat to medium-high, and cook for 10 minutes, stirring frequently. Top with crumbled bacon.

Sautéed Pears and Apples

Makes 6 servings

¼	cup butter
1	cup firmly packed light brown sugar
¼	cup honey
½	teaspoon ground cinnamon
¼	teaspoon salt
3	Granny Smith apples, cored and sliced into ¼-inch-thick slices
3	red Anjou pears, cored and sliced into ¼-inch-thick slices

1. In a large skillet, melt butter over medium heat. Add brown sugar, honey, cinnamon, and salt, stirring to combine. Add apples and pears; toss gently to coat with butter mixture. Cover and cook, stirring occasionally, for 10 minutes or until fruit begins to get tender. Uncover and increase heat to medium-high. Cook, stirring frequently, for 15 minutes or until syrup thickens and fruit is lightly browned.

Walnut-Crusted Chicken

Makes 6 servings

¼ cup olive oil
6 boneless skinless chicken breasts
1½ teaspoons salt, divided
½ teaspoon ground black pepper, divided
1 cup all-purpose flour
2 large eggs
2 tablespoons water
1 cup panko (Japanese breadcrumbs)
1 cup finely chopped walnuts
1 tablespoon finely chopped fresh thyme
Creamy Pumpkin Sauce (recipe follows)
Garnish: fresh thyme

1. Preheat oven to 375°. Line a rimmed baking sheet with aluminum foil. Brush foil with ¼ cup olive oil; set aside.

2. Season chicken with 1 teaspoon salt and ¼ teaspoon pepper.

3. In a shallow dish, combine flour, remaining ½ teaspoon salt, and remaining ¼ teaspoon pepper.

4. In a separate shallow dish, combine eggs and water; beat with a fork until well combined.

5. In another shallow dish, combine panko, walnuts, and thyme.

6. Coat chicken with flour mixture, shaking off excess. Dip floured chicken in egg mixture, allowing excess to drip off. Coat chicken in panko mixture. Place on prepared baking sheet.

7. Bake for 30 minutes. Turn chicken; bake for 30 minutes longer or until done. Serve with Creamy Pumpkin Sauce. Garnish with thyme, if desired.

CREAMY PUMPKIN SAUCE
Makes 2¼ cups

2 tablespoons butter
¼ cup minced shallot
2 tablespoons minced garlic
¼ cup dry white wine
1½ cups heavy whipping cream
1 cup pumpkin puree
¼ cup chicken broth
½ teaspoon salt
¼ teaspoon ground white pepper
¼ teaspoon ground black pepper
½ cup freshly grated Parmigiano-Reggiano cheese

1. In a medium saucepan, melt butter over medium heat. Add shallot and garlic; cook for 3 minutes. Add wine; cook for 2 minutes. Add cream, pumpkin puree, chicken broth, salt, white pepper, and black pepper. Cook for 5 minutes or until slightly thickened. Add cheese, stirring until cheese melts.

from heat, and cool for 10 minutes. Strain mixture through a fine-mesh strainer into an airtight container. Cover and chill for 4 hours to overnight.

4. Pour chilled mixture into an ice cream freezer, and freeze according to manufacturer's instructions. Transfer to an airtight freezer-safe container, and freeze until ready to serve. Top with Pecan Crumble Topping.

PECAN CRUMBLE TOPPING
Makes about 2 cups

1	cup all-purpose flour
⅓	cup firmly packed light brown sugar
½	teaspoon pumpkin pie spice
½	teaspoon ground cinnamon
½	cup chopped pecans
½	cup butter, melted

1. Preheat oven to 350°.

2. In a medium bowl, combine flour, brown sugar, pumpkin pie spice, and cinnamon. Stir in pecans. Add melted butter, stirring to combine. Spread mixture into an ungreased 13x9-inch baking pan. Bake for 15 to 20 minutes or until lightly browned, stirring occasionally to crumble. Let cool completely. Store in an airtight container.

Pumpkin-Pie Ice Cream
Makes about 1½ quarts

6	large egg yolks, lightly beaten
1½	cups pumpkin puree
1	tablespoon pumpkin pie spice
1	teaspoon ground cinnamon
1	teaspoon vanilla extract
2	(12-ounce) cans evaporated milk
1¾	cups heavy whipping cream
1¼	cups sugar
¼	teaspoon salt
Pecan Crumble Topping (recipe follows)	

1. In a medium bowl, combine egg yolks, pumpkin puree, pumpkin pie spice, cinnamon, and vanilla; set aside.

2. In a large saucepan, combine milk, cream, sugar, and salt. Heat over medium-low heat until milk mixture is barely simmering.

3. Pour one-fourth of hot milk mixture into yolk mixture, whisking constantly. Pour yolk mixture into remaining hot milk mixture, whisking constantly. Cook over medium heat, whisking constantly, until mixture thickens and coats the back of a spoon, about 5 minutes. Remove

Coastal HOLIDAY

Island rhythms, zesty spices, and oceanic accents unite for a seasonal salute that embraces the best of sea and shore.

Menu

TROPICAL AMBROSIA

CHORIZO-STUFFED PORK LOIN WITH CITRUS GLAZE

BROWN RICE PILAF WITH SPINACH

SAUTÉED PLANTAINS AND SWEET POTATOES

KEY LIME AND RASPBERRY DESSERT

When spending the holidays amid warmer weather, the sentiment behind the celebration remains the same, but the fare and festivities take on a flavor all their own. The back porch is a prime location for a coastal Christmas dinner, one that family and friends will dearly love. Exchange evergreen for palm leaves, and instead of pinecones and berries, use shells and coral to create a captivating scene. Muted colors and soft touches provide a sophisticated palette on which to present a palatable selection of vibrant Floribbean foods. Watching over the soiree, a cherub centerpiece sweetly bears glad tidings and encourages joy for one and all.

Sautéed Plantains and Sweet Potatoes

Makes 8 to 10 servings

3	quarts water
4	cups diced sweet potatoes (½-inch cubes)
1	cup butter, divided
4	plantains, peeled and diced
1	cup firmly packed light brown sugar
1	tablespoon fresh lemon juice
½	teaspoon ground cinnamon
½	teaspoon salt

1. In a Dutch oven, bring water to a boil over high heat. Add sweet potatoes. Return to a boil for 5 minutes or until just tender. Drain well.

2. In a large nonstick skillet, melt ½ cup butter over medium heat. Add sweet potatoes and plantains. Cook, turning occasionally with a spatula, until lightly browned, about 20 minutes. Remove from pan; set aside.

3. In same skillet, melt remaining ½ cup butter over medium heat. Add brown sugar, lemon juice, cinnamon, and salt; cook for 2 minutes, stirring constantly.

Return sweet potatoes and plantains to skillet, tossing gently to coat with sauce. Cook until heated through.

Brown Rice Pilaf with Spinach

Makes 8 to 10 servings

¼	cup butter
1	cup chopped yellow onion
1	tablespoon minced garlic
1	(16-ounce) box whole-grain brown rice
½	teaspoon ground black pepper
5	cups chicken broth
1	(9-ounce) bag fresh spinach, stemmed and chopped

1. In a Dutch oven, melt butter over medium-high heat. Add onion and garlic; cook for 3 minutes, stirring constantly. Add rice and pepper; cook for 5 minutes, stirring constantly.

2. Add broth. Bring to a boil; reduce heat to low, cover, and cook for 20 minutes.

3. Add spinach, stirring to combine. Cover and cook, stirring occasionally, until all liquid is absorbed, about 6 to 8 minutes. Remove from heat. Let rice stand, covered, for 5 minutes. Fluff with a fork before serving.

Chorizo-Stuffed Pork Loin

Makes 8 to 10 servings

6	tablespoons olive oil, divided
1	tablespoon minced garlic
2	cups chopped chorizo
1	cup fresh or frozen corn kernels
¾	cup chopped green onion
½	cup chopped red bell pepper
½	cup canned black beans
3	tablespoons chopped fresh parsley
2	tablespoons fresh lime juice
¾	teaspoon salt, divided
¾	teaspoon ground black pepper, divided
1½	cups fresh breadcrumbs
1	(5-pound) boneless pork loin, trimmed

Citrus Glaze (recipe follows)

1. In a large skillet, heat 4 tablespoons olive oil over medium heat. Add garlic; cook for 1 minute, stirring constantly. Add chorizo, corn, green onion, bell pepper, black beans, parsley, lime juice, ¼ teaspoon salt, and ¼ teaspoon pepper. Cook for 10 minutes, stirring frequently. Remove from heat. Add breadcrumbs, stirring to combine. Set aside.

2. Preheat oven to 475°.

3. Place pork loin on a clean surface. Cut into one long side of loin, leaving a ½-inch border; continue cutting in a circular pattern until loin can be rolled out into a rectangle that is about ½-inch thick. Top with heavy-duty plastic wrap. Using a meat mallet, pound pork to an even ½-inch thickness. Spread chorizo mixture over pork, leaving a 1-inch border.

4. Starting at a long side, roll up pork, jelly-roll style. Secure at 2-inch intervals with butcher's twine. Rub outside of stuffed pork loin with remaining 2 tablespoons olive oil, and sprinkle

with remaining ½ teaspoon salt and remaining ½ teaspoon pepper. Place, seam side down, in a roasting pan. Bake for 20 minutes.

5. Reduce oven temperature to 325°. Pour Citrus Glaze over pork loin; loosely cover with aluminum foil. Bake for 30 to 40 minutes or until a meat thermometer inserted into center of pork loin reaches 150°, basting occasionally. Let rest for 10 minutes. Spoon glaze from pan over pork loin before serving.

CITRUS GLAZE

Makes about 1 cup

2	tablespoons butter
1	tablespoon minced garlic
1	tablespoon orange zest
1	tablespoon lime zest
1	tablespoon lemon zest
½	cup fresh orange juice
¼	cup firmly packed light brown sugar
2	tablespoons fresh lemon juice
2	tablespoons fresh lime juice
2	tablespoons honey
1	teaspoon Caribbean Jerk Seasoning

1. In a medium saucepan, melt butter over medium heat. Add garlic, orange

zest, lime zest, and lemon zest; cook for 2 minutes, stirring constantly. Add remaining ingredients, stirring until well combined. Reduce heat to low; bring to a simmer, and cook for 10 minutes, stirring frequently.

Tropical Ambrosia

Makes 8 to 10 servings

2	cups diced fresh pineapple (1-inch cubes)
2	cups diced fresh mango (1-inch cubes)
2	cups diced fresh papaya (1-inch cubes)
2	cups orange sections
½	cup cream of coconut
¼	cup fresh orange juice

Garnish: chopped toasted macadamia nuts, toasted flaked coconut

1. In a large bowl, combine pineapple, mango, papaya, and orange sections.

2. In a small bowl, combine cream of coconut and orange juice. Add to fruit mixture, tossing gently to coat. Cover and chill for 1 hour. Garnish with macadamia nuts and coconut, if desired.

Key Lime and Raspberry Dessert

Makes 1 (9-inch) dessert

Crust:
- 2 cups firmly packed graham cracker crumbs
- ⅓ cup sugar
- 6 tablespoons butter, melted

Filling:
- ¼ cup cold water
- 1 (0.25-ounce) envelope unflavored gelatin
- 2 (8-ounce) packages cream cheese, softened
- ⅓ cup Key lime juice
- ¼ cup unsalted butter, softened
- 3 tablespoons Key lime or lime zest
- 2 cups confectioners' sugar
- 1¼ cups heavy whipping cream
- 2 pints fresh raspberries
- ¼ cup seedless raspberry preserves, melted

Garnish: white chocolate curls, lime zest

1. **To prepare crust:** Preheat oven to 300°. In a small bowl, combine cracker crumbs, sugar, and melted butter. Press firmly on bottom and halfway up sides of a 9-inch springform pan. Bake for 8 minutes; set aside to cool.

2. **To prepare filling:** In a small microwave-safe bowl, combine water and gelatin; let stand for 2 minutes. Microwave on High for 30 seconds or until gelatin dissolves; let cool slightly.

3. In a large bowl, combine cream cheese, Key lime juice, butter, and lime zest. Beat at medium speed with an electric mixer until creamy. Gradually add confectioners' sugar, beating until combined.

4. In a separate bowl, beat cream at high speed until soft peaks form. Add gelatin mixture, beating until stiff peaks form. Fold mixture into cream cheese mixture. Spread in prepared crust. Cover with plastic wrap, and chill for 4 hours.

5. Remove plastic wrap, and run a knife around edge of pan. Carefully unlatch ring, and remove. Arrange raspberries over cream cheese mixture. Brush top with melted preserves. Garnish with white chocolate curls and zest, if desired.

BEST
RECIPES

CREAMY CHEESE GRITS WITH SAVORY SHRIMP, PAGE 134

1
Scrumptious
APPETIZERS AND BEVERAGES

Make a delicious first impression by welcoming guests with a tantalizing array of starters. Savory hors d'oeuvres paired with refreshing sippers allow partygoers to mix and mingle while whetting their appetites for the dinner to come— though some of these scrumptious appetizers are hearty enough to make a meal all on their own.

Deviled Eggs

Makes 2 dozen

12   large eggs
6   tablespoons mayonnaise
¼   cup sweet pickle relish
1   tablespoon country-style Dijon mustard
2   teaspoons dill pickle juice
1½   teaspoons prepared mustard
1   teaspoon Dijon mustard
¼   teaspoon celery seed
¼   teaspoon ground black pepper
Garnish: chopped green onion, paprika

1. Place eggs in a large saucepan with enough cold water to cover; cook over high heat until water begins to boil. Reduce heat to medium; simmer eggs for 10 minutes. Remove eggs from heat; drain eggs, and rinse with cold water. Peel eggs, discarding shells. Halve eggs lengthwise.

2. Remove yolks, and place in a small bowl. Mash yolks with fork until crumbly. Add mayonnaise, pickle relish, country-style Dijon mustard, dill pickle juice, mustard, Dijon mustard, celery seed, and pepper. Stir yolk mixture until well combined. Spoon yolk mixture evenly into egg whites. Garnish with green onion and paprika, if desired.

Avocado and Tomato Salsa

Makes about 6½ cups

3   cups chopped fresh tomatoes
2½   cups diced avocado
½   cup chopped red onion
1   yellow bell pepper, seeded and chopped
1   poblano chile pepper, seeded and chopped
1   bunch fresh cilantro, stems removed and chopped
¼   cup fresh lime juice
1   tablespoon hot sauce or to taste
1   teaspoon minced garlic
1   teaspoon salt
¼   teaspoon ground black pepper
Large avocados, halved and pitted (optional)

1. Combine first 11 ingredients in a large bowl, tossing gently to mix well. Cover and chill for 2 hours to allow flavors to meld.

2. To make avocado serving bowls: Using a teaspoon or melon baller, scoop out pulp of avocado halves, leaving ¼-inch-thick shells. Discard avocado pulp or reserve for another use. Spoon salsa into avocado halves. Serve salsa with tortilla chips.

Prosciutto and Brie Dip

Makes 10 to 12 servings

1   cup sour cream
1   (8-ounce) package cream cheese, softened
3   (5-ounce) containers crème de Brie*
½   cup grated Parmesan cheese
1½   cups chopped prosciutto, (about 6 ounces)
¼   cup chopped green onion
½   teaspoon red pepper flakes

1. Preheat oven to 375°. In a large bowl, combine sour cream, cream cheese, crème de Brie, and Parmesan cheese. Beat at medium speed with an electric mixer until smooth. Add prosciutto, green onion, and red pepper flakes, beating to combine. Spoon mixture into an 8-inch square baking dish. Bake for 15 to 20 minutes or until bubbly. Serve with crackers or Melba toast rounds.

*If crème de Brie is not available, 15 ounces of softened Brie with rind removed may be substituted.

Fresh Spinach and Artichoke Dip

Makes about 6 cups

2   tablespoons olive oil
2   teaspoons minced garlic
2   (6-ounce) packages fresh baby spinach
2   (8-ounce) packages cream cheese, softened
2   (16-ounce) containers sour cream
1   (1-ounce) package ranch-flavored dip mix
½   teaspoon freshly ground black pepper
1   (14-ounce) can artichoke hearts, drained and chopped
½   cup chopped green onion
Garnish: chopped green onion

1. In a large Dutch oven, heat olive oil over medium heat. Add minced garlic, and cook for 1 to 2 minutes, stirring constantly, until lightly browned. Add spinach; cook for 3 to 4 minutes, stirring constantly, until wilted. Cool completely; drain spinach, and finely chop.

2. In a large bowl, combine cream cheese, sour cream, ranch-flavored dip mix, and pepper. Add spinach, artichoke hearts, and green onion, mixing well. Cover and chill for 2 hours. Garnish with chopped green onion, if desired. Serve with crackers.

Mini Potato Skins with Horseradish Dipping Sauce

Makes 2 dozen

Potato skins:

12	small red potatoes, washed and dried
3	tablespoons olive oil, divided
1	teaspoon Creole seasoning
½	teaspoon salt
¼	teaspoon ground black pepper
1½	cups shredded Cheddar and Monterey Jack cheese blend
8	slices bacon, cooked and crumbled
¼	cup chopped green onion

Sauce:

1	cup sour cream
½	cup mayonnaise
2	tablespoons prepared horseradish
1	tablespoon chopped fresh chives
¼	teaspoon salt
¼	teaspoon ground black pepper

Garnish: sliced fresh chives

1. To prepare potato skins: Preheat oven to 375°. Line a baking sheet with aluminum foil. Rub potatoes with 1 tablespoon olive oil to coat skins. Place on prepared baking sheet. Bake for 45 minutes or until done.

2. Cool potatoes until easy to handle. Cut potatoes in half; using a teaspoon or melon baller, scoop out pulp, leaving ¼-inch-thick shells. Discard potato pulp or reserve for another use.

3. In a small bowl, combine remaining 2 tablespoons oil, Creole seasoning, salt, and pepper. Brush inside of potatoes with oil mixture. Bake for 15 minutes. Top with cheese, bacon, and green onion; bake for 5 minutes longer or until cheese melts.

4. To prepare sauce: Combine all ingredients (except garnish) in a small bowl. Cover and chill until ready to serve. Garnish with sliced chives, if desired. Serve with potato skins.

Johnny Cakes with Tomato-Corn Relish

Makes 1½ dozen

Relish:

2	tablespoons butter
1	cup fresh or frozen corn kernels
½	cup chopped fresh or frozen okra
½	cup finely chopped red bell pepper
¼	cup finely chopped yellow bell pepper
¼	cup chopped green onion
2	teaspoons minced garlic
½	cup seeded chopped tomato
2	teaspoons sugar
1	teaspoon fresh lemon juice
½	teaspoon salt
¼	teaspoon ground red pepper

Cakes:

1	cup yellow cornmeal
½	cup all-purpose flour
1	tablespoon chopped fresh parsley
¾	teaspoon salt
½	teaspoon ground black pepper
1	cup finely grated Gruyère cheese
1½	cups milk
¼	cup butter, melted
1	large egg, lightly beaten

Butter for frying

Garnish: cooked crumbled bacon, chopped fresh parsley

1. To prepare relish: In a medium skillet, melt butter over medium heat. Add corn, okra, red bell pepper, yellow bell pepper, green onion, and garlic. Cook for 4 to 5 minutes, stirring frequently, until tender. Add tomato, sugar, lemon juice, salt, and red pepper. Cook for 2 minutes, stirring frequently, until tender. Keep warm.

2. To prepare cakes: In a medium bowl, combine cornmeal, flour, parsley, salt, and pepper. Add cheese, stirring to combine. In a small bowl, combine milk, butter, and egg. Add milk mixture to cornmeal mixture, stirring to combine.

3. In a nonstick skillet, melt 1 tablespoon butter over medium heat. Working in batches, spoon about 2 tablespoons cornmeal mixture for each cake into hot skillet. Fry for 2 to 3 minutes per side or until golden brown. Repeat procedure with additional butter and remaining cornmeal mixture. Top cakes with relish. Garnish with bacon and parsley, if desired.

Creamy Cheese Grits with Savory Shrimp

Makes 8 to 10 servings

Grits:

10	cups chicken broth
2	cups stone-ground grits
1	cup heavy whipping cream
½	cup butter
½	teaspoon ground black pepper
¼	teaspoon ground red pepper
2	cups grated fontina cheese
1	cup grated Gruyère cheese

Rémoulade:

½	cup mayonnaise
2	tablespoons chopped green onion
2	tablespoons sweet pickle relish
1	tablespoon Creole mustard
1	tablespoon ketchup
1	tablespoon chopped fresh parsley
2	teaspoons capers, rinsed and drained
1½	teaspoons prepared horseradish
½	teaspoon minced garlic
½	teaspoon hot pepper sauce
½	teaspoon Worcestershire sauce
¼	teaspoon ground black pepper

Caramelized onions:

¼	cup butter
2	large yellow onions, sliced ⅛ inch thick
1	tablespoon balsamic vinegar
½	teaspoon salt
¼	teaspoon ground black pepper

Shrimp:

2	tablespoons butter
2	tablespoons olive oil
½	cup finely chopped red bell pepper
½	cup finely chopped green onion
1	tablespoon Creole seasoning
2	teaspoons minced garlic
¼	teaspoon ground black pepper
½	cup dry white wine
2	pounds peeled and deveined fresh large shrimp, tails on
1	tablespoon chopped fresh parsley
1	tablespoon fresh lemon juice

1. **To prepare grits:** In a large Dutch oven, bring chicken broth to a boil. Stir in grits; return to a boil over medium heat, stirring constantly. Reduce heat to low. Simmer for 2 hours, stirring occasionally, until creamy. Add cream, butter, black pepper, and red pepper. Cook for 30 minutes, stirring frequently. Stir in cheeses.

2. **To prepare rémoulade:** Combine all ingredients in the work bowl of a food processor. Process until well blended. Cover and refrigerate until ready to serve.

3. **To prepare caramelized onions:** In a large skillet, melt butter over medium-low heat. Add onions; cover and cook for 30 minutes, stirring occasionally. Remove cover, and increase heat to medium-high. Add vinegar, salt, and pepper. Cook for 10 minutes, stirring constantly, until golden brown.

4. **To prepare shrimp:** In a large skillet, melt butter with olive oil over medium heat. Add bell pepper, green onion, Creole seasoning, garlic, and pepper. Cook for 2 minutes, stirring constantly. Add wine; cook for 2 minutes. Increase heat to medium-high. Add shrimp; cook, stirring constantly, for 2 to 3 minutes or until shrimp are just pink. Add parsley and lemon juice, stirring to combine.

5. **To serve:** Place shrimp, grits, onions, and rémoulade in separate serving bowls. Set out martini glasses or small bowls for individual serving dishes.

Hoppin' John Egg Rolls with Spicy Peach Dipping Sauce

Makes 15 egg rolls

Egg rolls:
2	tablespoons bacon drippings
1	cup chopped onion
½	cup chopped red bell pepper
2	teaspoons minced garlic
½	teaspoon salt
¼	teaspoon ground black pepper
1	(8-ounce) package diced cooked ham
1	(15.8-ounce) can black-eyed peas, drained
2	cups cooked rice
2	tablespoons chopped fresh parsley
1	(1-pound) package egg roll wrappers
1	large egg, lightly beaten

Vegetable oil for frying

Sauce:
1	tablespoon butter
1	teaspoon minced garlic
1	jalapeño pepper, seeded and minced
1	(18-ounce) jar peach preserves
2	tablespoons fresh lemon juice
1	tablespoon Creole mustard
¼	teaspoon salt

1. To prepare egg rolls: In a large skillet, heat bacon drippings over medium heat. Add onion, bell pepper, garlic, salt, and pepper; cook for 3 minutes or until vegetables are tender. Add ham, black-eyed peas, and rice. Cook for 2 to 3 minutes, stirring constantly. Add parsley, stirring to combine. Remove from heat, and cool slightly.

2. Spoon about 4 tablespoons filling on bottom one-third of an egg roll wrapper. Fold the lower corner over filling, and roll it up about one-third of the way. Brush the left and right corners of wrapper with beaten egg; fold corners toward center of filling. Brush top edge with egg, and roll up tightly; repeat for each roll.

3. In a Dutch oven, pour oil to a depth of 2 inches; heat to 350°.

4. Fry egg rolls, in batches, for 2 to 3 minutes or until golden brown. Drain on paper towels.

5. To prepare sauce: In a small saucepan, melt butter over medium-high heat. Add garlic and jalapeño pepper; cook for 2 minutes. Reduce heat to medium-low. Add peach preserves, lemon juice, mustard, and salt, stirring to combine. Simmer for 5 minutes, stirring frequently. Serve sauce with egg rolls.

Pecan Pie Tartlets

Makes about 3 dozen

Crust:
- ½ cup sugar
- ¼ cup butter, softened
- 1 (3-ounce) package cream cheese, softened
- 1 large egg
- 1¾ cups all-purpose flour

Filling:
- ⅓ cup light corn syrup
- ⅓ cup dark corn syrup
- ½ cup sugar
- 2 tablespoons butter, melted and cooled
- 2 large eggs, lightly beaten
- 1 teaspoon vanilla extract
- ¾ cup finely chopped pecans

1. To prepare crust: In a medium bowl, combine sugar, butter, and cream cheese. Beat at medium speed with an electric mixer until smooth. Add egg, beating until smooth. Gradually add flour. Beat at low speed until just combined; dough will be sticky. Cover and chill dough for 1 hour.

2. Preheat oven to 350°. Roll dough into 1-inch balls; press in bottom and two-thirds up sides of each cup of miniature muffin pans.

3. To prepare filling: In a medium bowl, combine corn syrups, sugar, melted butter, eggs, and vanilla, whisking to combine.

4. Spoon corn syrup mixture into each prepared crust. Top with chopped pecans. Bake for 18 to 20 minutes or until lightly browned.

Kahlúa and Coffee Fudge

Makes 10 to 12 servings

- 1 (14-ounce) can sweetened condensed milk
- ¼ cup Kahlúa
- 2 tablespoons instant coffee granules
- 1 (12-ounce) package semisweet chocolate morsels
- 1 cup chopped pecans
- ½ teaspoon vanilla extract

1. Line an 8-inch square baking pan with aluminum foil. In a large, heavy-duty saucepan, combine condensed milk, Kahlúa, and coffee granules over medium heat. Bring to a simmer; cook for 2 minutes, stirring constantly, until mixture thickens slightly. Remove from heat, and stir in chocolate morsels until melted and smooth. Stir in pecans and vanilla.

2. Spread evenly into prepared baking pan. Refrigerate for 2 hours. Remove from pan by lifting foil. Peel back foil, and cut fudge into squares to serve.

Amaretto Cheesecake Squares

Makes 2 dozen

1¾ cups all-purpose flour, divided
½ cup firmly packed light brown sugar
½ cup butter, melted
2 (8-ounce) packages cream cheese, softened
½ cup sugar
4 large eggs
¼ cup amaretto liqueur
½ teaspoon almond extract
⅓ cup sliced almonds

1. Preheat oven to 350°. Combine 1½ cups flour, brown sugar, and melted butter. Press firmly in bottom of a 13x9-inch baking pan. Bake for 6 to 8 minutes.

2. In a large bowl, combine cream cheese, sugar, and remaining ¼ cup flour. Beat at medium speed with an electric mixer until well combined. Add eggs, one at a time, beating well after each addition. Add amaretto and almond extract, beating to combine.

3. Spread filling over prepared crust; sprinkle with sliced almonds. Bake for 25 minutes or until set. Cool completely. Cover and refrigerate for 2 hours to overnight; cut into squares.

Lemon Chess Buttermilk Tartlets

Makes 2 dozen

1 (14.1-ounce) box refrigerated pie crust
¾ cup sugar
2 tablespoons all-purpose flour
1 tablespoon lemon zest
⅔ cup whole buttermilk
3 egg yolks
¼ cup butter, melted and cooled
½ teaspoon vanilla extract
Garnish: whipped cream, lemon zest, fresh mint sprigs

1. Preheat oven to 350°. Spray a 24-count mini muffin pan with nonstick baking spray with flour.

2. Using a 2¾-inch round cutter, cut 12 circles from each pie crust. Press crusts into bottom and up sides of each muffin cup.

3. In a medium bowl, combine sugar, flour, and lemon zest. In a separate bowl, combine buttermilk, egg yolks, butter, and vanilla, whisking to combine. Add buttermilk mixture to sugar mixture, stirring to combine well. Spoon about 1 tablespoon mixture into each prepared crust. Bake for 18 to 20 minutes or until set. Remove from oven, and cool. Garnish with whipped cream, lemon zest, and mint, if desired.

Lemonade

Makes 1½ quarts

6   cups water, divided
2   cups sugar
1   bunch lemon balm
Juice of 2 large lemons
Garnish: lemon balm, lemon slices

1. In a medium saucepan, combine 3 cups water with sugar. Bring to a boil over medium heat; reduce heat, and simmer until sugar is dissolved. Remove from heat; add lemon balm, cover, and let sit until cool.

2. Strain mixture into a large pitcher. Add remaining 3 cups water and lemon juice. To serve, pour into chilled glasses, and garnish with lemon balm and lemon slices, if desired.

Lemon-Mint Tea

Makes about 1 gallon

3½   quarts cold water, divided
3   family-size tea bags
½   cup fresh mint leaves
1½   cups sugar
1   (12-ounce) can frozen pink lemonade
     concentrate, thawed
Garnish: lemon slices

1. In a medium saucepan, bring 1 quart water to a boil; remove from heat. Add tea bags and mint; cover and steep for 5 minutes.

2. Strain tea into a large container. Add sugar, stirring until sugar is dissolved. Add lemonade concentrate and remaining water; stir to mix well. Serve over ice. Garnish with lemon slices, if desired.

Note: Fresh mint sprigs also make a nice addition to this beverage.

Cherry Limeade

Makes about ½ gallon

3   cups water
1   cup fresh lime juice
1   cup sugar
¾   cup maraschino cherry juice
4   cups lemon-lime-flavored
      carbonated beverage, chilled
Garnish: lime slices, maraschino cherries,
      fresh mint sprigs

1. In a large pitcher, combine water, lime juice, sugar, and maraschino cherry juice. Stir until sugar dissolves. Chill until ready to serve.

2. Slowly add lemon-lime-flavored carbonated beverage to pitcher, stirring gently to combine. Serve immediately over ice. Garnish with lime slices, cherries, and fresh mint, if desired.

Party Punch

Makes about 5 quarts

1   (46-ounce) can pineapple juice
1   (32-ounce) bottle cranberry juice
      cocktail
1   (12-ounce) can frozen lemonade
      concentrate, thawed
1   (2-liter) bottle ginger ale, chilled
Garnish: orange slices

1. In a large pitcher, combine pineapple juice, cranberry juice cocktail, and lemonade concentrate. Chill until ready to serve.

2. Slowly add ginger ale, stirring gently to combine. Serve immediately. Garnish with orange slices, if desired.

Frozen Watermelon Daiquiri

Makes 2 drinks

2   cups seeded and diced watermelon, frozen
4   ounces watermelon-flavored rum
3   ounces Simple Syrup (recipe follows)
1½ ounces fresh lime juice
Garnish: watermelon wedges

1. Combine all ingredients (except garnish) in the container of a blender; process until smooth. Garnish with watermelon wedges, if desired.

SIMPLE SYRUP
Makes 1½ cups

1   cup sugar
1   cup water

1. In a small saucepan, combine sugar and water over medium-high heat, stirring constantly. Bring mixture to a boil; reduce heat to low, and simmer for 3 to 4 minutes, stirring constantly. Remove from heat, and cool completely. Pour into an airtight container. Store syrup in refrigerator for up to 3 weeks.

Sunrise Smoothie

Makes 6 servings

2¼ cups orange juice
2¼ cups vanilla ice cream or frozen vanilla yogurt
1½ cups frozen strawberry sorbet
Garnish: fresh strawberries

1. Combine all ingredients (except garnish) in container of a blender; puree until smooth. Pour into glasses. Garnish with fresh strawberries, if desired.

Sparkling Brunch Punch

Makes about 1½ gallons

1   (46-ounce) can pineapple juice
6   cups orange juice
1   (12-ounce) can frozen lemonade concentrate, thawed
1   (750-milliliter) bottle sparkling white grape juice, chilled
1   (2-liter) bottle lemon-lime-flavored carbonated beverage, chilled
Garnish: orange slices

1. In a large bowl, combine pineapple juice, orange juice, and lemonade concentrate.

2. When ready to serve, add sparkling white grape juice and lemon-lime-flavored carbonated beverage, stirring gently to combine. Garnish with orange slices, if desired.

Milk Punch

Makes about 1 gallon

½   gallon milk
1½   cups bourbon
¼   cup sugar
1   teaspoon vanilla extract
1   quart vanilla ice cream, softened
Garnish: ground nutmeg

1. In a large pitcher, combine milk, bourbon, sugar, and vanilla, stirring until sugar is dissolved. Add ice cream, stirring to combine. Cover and chill. Garnish with nutmeg, if desired.

Cranberry-Pomegranate Cider

Makes 1 gallon

1   (64-ounce) bottle cranberry juice
    cocktail
1   (64-ounce) bottle pomegranate juice
¾   cup sugar
1   tablespoon whole cloves
1   orange, sliced
Garnish: orange slices, cloves

1. Combine all ingredients (except garnish) in a large Dutch oven. Bring to a simmer over medium heat, and cook for 20 minutes; remove cloves. Garnish with orange slices and cloves, if desired.

Hot Rum Punch

Makes about 3 quarts

1   (64-ounce) bottle apple cider
½   cup sugar
3   cinnamon sticks
1   tablespoon whole cloves
2   cups fresh orange juice
1   cup light rum
½   cup fresh lemon juice
Garnish: orange slices, cloves

1. In a Dutch oven over medium heat, combine apple cider, sugar, cinnamon sticks, and cloves. Simmer, uncovered, for 10 minutes; remove spices, and discard. Add orange juice, rum, and lemon juice. Garnish with orange slices and cloves, if desired.

Hot Caramel Cocoa

Makes about 2 quarts

4   (1-ounce) squares unsweetened
    chocolate, chopped
1   cup heavy whipping cream
4   cups milk
1   (12-ounce) can evaporated milk
½   cup firmly packed light brown sugar
1   cup caramel-flavored liqueur
Garnish: whipped cream, caramel topping

1. In a small microwave-safe bowl, microwave chocolate and cream on High, in 30-second intervals, stirring between each, until smooth (about 1½ minutes total).

2. In a large Dutch oven, combine milk, evaporated milk, and brown sugar. Cook over medium heat, stirring until sugar dissolves. Add chocolate mixture, whisking until smooth. Bring to a simmer. Reduce heat to low, and add liqueur. Garnish servings with whipped cream and caramel topping, if desired.

Spiced Fruit Cider

Makes about 2½ quarts

6   cups apple cider
4   cups pomegranate juice
4   cups cranberry juice cocktail
½   cup fresh lemon juice
½   cup sugar
4   whole cinnamon sticks
2   tablespoons whole cloves
2   tablespoons whole allspice
4   pieces candied ginger
Garnish: cinnamon sticks

1. In a Dutch oven, combine apple cider, pomegranate juice, cranberry juice, lemon juice, and sugar. Cook over medium heat, stirring until sugar dissolves. Add cinnamon sticks, cloves, allspice, and ginger. Simmer, uncovered, for 1 hour; remove spices. Garnish with cinnamon sticks, if desired.

CLOVERLEAF ROLLS, PAGE 153

2
Enticing
BREADS

Crispy, crumbly, flaky, tender—whether it's buttery rolls hot from the oven or melt-in-your-mouth biscuits filled with homemade peach preserves, bread is an oh-so delectable component of any meal. Besides, the enticing aroma of bread baking is positively irresistible!

Baby Biscuits

Makes about 2 dozen

2   **cups self-rising flour**
½   **cup shortening**
½   **cup milk**
2   **tablespoons butter, melted**

1. Preheat oven to 425°. Lightly grease a baking sheet.

2. Place flour in a medium bowl. Using a pastry blender, cut in shortening until mixture is crumbly. Add milk, stirring just until dry ingredients are moistened.

3. On a floured surface, roll dough to ½-inch thickness. Using a 1½-inch round cutter, cut biscuits, and place ½ inch apart on prepared baking sheet. Bake for 12 to 14 minutes or until lightly browned. Brush with melted butter. Serve with peach preserves, if desired.

Cheddar-Green Olive Biscuits

Makes about 1½ dozen

2   **cups self-rising flour**
½   **cup butter**
1   **cup finely grated sharp Cheddar cheese**
¾   **cup finely chopped green olives**
⅔   **cup half-and-half**
2   **tablespoons butter, melted**

1. Preheat oven to 425°. Lightly grease a baking sheet.

2. Place flour in a medium bowl. Using a pastry blender, cut in ½ cup butter until mixture is crumbly. Add cheese and olives; stir to combine well. Add half-and-half, stirring just until dry ingredients are moistened.

3. On a floured surface, roll dough to ½-inch thickness. Using a 2-inch round cutter, cut biscuits, and place on prepared baking sheet. Bake for 13 to 15 minutes or until lightly browned. Brush with melted butter.

Parker House Rolls

Makes about 3 dozen

2	(¼-ounce) packages active dry yeast
½	cup sugar, divided
2	cups warm milk (105° to 110°)
7	cups bread flour
1	tablespoon salt
1	cup vegetable oil
2	large eggs, lightly beaten
½	cup butter, melted and divided

1. In a small bowl, combine yeast, ¼ cup sugar, and warm milk; let stand for 5 minutes or until foamy.

2. In a small bowl, combine bread flour, remaining ¼ cup sugar, and salt.

3. In the bowl of a stand mixer fitted with a dough hook attachment, combine milk mixture, oil, and eggs. Gradually add flour mixture to milk mixture, beating at medium speed until it forms a soft dough.

4. Turn dough out onto a lightly floured surface; knead until smooth and elastic, about 5 minutes. Place dough in a large greased bowl, turning to grease top. Loosely cover, and let rise in a warm place (85°), free from drafts, for 1 to 1½ hours or until doubled in size. Punch dough down; cover and let stand for 10 minutes.

5. Brush 3 baking sheets with melted butter; set aside. On a lightly floured surface, roll dough to ½-inch thickness. Cut with a 2½-inch round cutter; do not reroll scraps (see Cloverleaf Rolls below).

6. To shape, use a wooden spoon handle to make a slightly off-center crease in each round. Fold small half over large half, overlapping slightly. Press folded edge firmly. Place rolls, 3 inches apart, on prepared baking sheets. Brush with melted butter. Cover and let rise in a warm place (85°), free from drafts, for 1 hour or until doubled in size.

7. Preheat oven to 375°. Uncover rolls, and bake for 13 to 15 minutes or until lightly browned. Brush with remaining melted butter.

More to Love CLOVERLEAF ROLLS

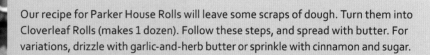

Our recipe for Parker House Rolls will leave some scraps of dough. Turn them into Cloverleaf Rolls (makes 1 dozen). Follow these steps, and spread with butter. For variations, drizzle with garlic-and-herb butter or sprinkle with cinnamon and sugar.

1. For cloverleaf rolls, grease a 12-cup muffin pan. Shape dough scraps into 1-inch balls, and place 3 dough balls in each muffin cup. Cover and let rise in a warm place (85°), free from drafts, for 1 to 1½ hours or until doubled in size.

2. Preheat oven to 350°. Uncover rolls, and bake for 15 minutes or until lightly browned.

Easy Garlic Rolls

Makes 6 rolls

¼   cup butter, melted and cooled
1   tablespoon chopped fresh parsley
½   teaspoon garlic salt
Frozen yeast roll dough, thawed

1. In a small bowl, combine melted butter, parsley, and garlic salt; set aside.

2. Cut 18 (1-inch) pieces of dough. Roll each piece of dough in butter mixture. Place 3 balls into each cup of a 6-cup muffin pan. Cover and let rise in a warm place (85°), free from drafts, until doubled in size, about 2 hours.

3. Preheat oven to 375°. Uncover rolls, and bake for 13 to 15 minutes or until golden brown.

Garlic Cheddar Muffins

Makes 1 dozen

1   tablespoon olive oil
¼   cup butter
¼   cup chopped fresh chives
1½ teaspoons minced garlic
2   cups baking mix
1   cup grated extra-sharp Cheddar cheese
¼   teaspoon garlic powder
¼   teaspoon ground black pepper
1   cup buttermilk

1. Preheat oven to 350°. Grease a 12-cup muffin pan with olive oil.

2. In a small saucepan, melt butter over medium heat. Add chives and garlic, and cook for 2 minutes; remove from heat, and set aside.

3. In a medium bowl, combine baking mix, cheese, garlic powder, and pepper. In a separate bowl, combine buttermilk and butter mixture. Add buttermilk mixture to cheese mixture, stirring until dry ingredients are moistened. Let batter stand for 5 minutes.

4. Evenly spoon batter into prepared muffin pan. Bake for 30 minutes or until golden brown. Cool in pan for 5 minutes.

Peach Melba French Toast

Makes 4 servings

½   cup peach preserves
3   medium peaches, finely chopped
8   (1-inch-thick) slices white bread
2   large eggs
1   (12-ounce) can evaporated milk
¼   cup sugar
¼   teaspoon ground cinnamon
2   tablespoons butter, divided
Raspberry Syrup (recipe follows)
Garnish: confectioners' sugar

1. In a small microwave-safe bowl, microwave peach preserves on High for about 1 minute or until preserves melt. Add peaches; stir to mix well.

2. Slice bread horizontally almost in half, leaving one edge intact. Spread peach mixture inside each piece of sliced bread (do not overstuff).

3. Whisk together eggs, milk, sugar, and cinnamon. In a 12-inch nonstick skillet over medium-low heat, melt 1 tablespoon butter. Dip 4 pieces of stuffed bread in egg mixture to coat both sides. Cook slices until golden brown, about 5 minutes on each side. Repeat procedure with remaining 4 slices. Serve with warm Raspberry Syrup. Garnish with confectioners' sugar, if desired.

RASPBERRY SYRUP
Makes about 1½ cups

1   cup fresh or frozen raspberries
½   cup light corn syrup
¼   cup sugar

1. In a small saucepan, combine raspberries, corn syrup, and sugar; bring to a boil, stirring frequently. Reduce heat to low, and simmer for 10 minutes.

Lemon Pancakes with Fresh Blueberry Syrup

Makes 6 servings

1½   **cups all-purpose flour**
2   **tablespoons sugar**
2   **teaspoons baking powder**
1½   **cups buttermilk**
2   **large eggs, lightly beaten**
2   **tablespoons butter, melted**
2   **tablespoons lemon zest**
2   **tablespoons fresh lemon juice**
4   **tablespoons butter, divided**
Fresh Blueberry Syrup (recipe follows)
Garnish: lemon slices

1. In a medium bowl, combine flour, sugar, and baking powder.

2. In a separate bowl, combine buttermilk, eggs, melted butter, zest, and juice. Add to flour mixture. Beat at medium speed with an electric mixer until smooth.

3. In a large nonstick skillet, melt 1 tablespoon butter over medium heat. Spoon 2 tablespoons batter for each pancake into skillet. Cook for 1 to 2 minutes per side or until lightly browned. Repeat with remaining butter and pancake batter. Serve with warm Fresh Blueberry Syrup. Garnish with lemon slices, if desired.

FRESH BLUEBERRY SYRUP
Makes 2 cups

1   **cup water**
1   **cup sugar**
¼   **cup light corn syrup**
1   **tablespoon fresh lemon juice**
2   **cups fresh blueberries**

1. In a medium saucepan, combine water, sugar, corn syrup, and lemon juice over medium-high heat. Bring to a simmer, stirring frequently, until sugar is dissolved.

2. Add blueberries; cook for 15 to 20 minutes or until syrupy, stirring occasionally. Cool slightly before serving.

Mexican Cornbread

Makes 10 to 12 servings

2	tablespoons butter
1	cup fresh corn kernels
¾	cup finely chopped green onion
¾	cup finely chopped red bell pepper
1	tablespoon vegetable shortening
2	cups yellow self-rising cornmeal mix
½	cup self-rising flour
2	teaspoons sugar
1	teaspoon salt
¾	cup grated Monterey Jack cheese with peppers
2	cups whole buttermilk
4	tablespoons butter, melted
1	large egg, lightly beaten

1. Preheat oven to 425°.

2. In a medium skillet, melt 2 tablespoons butter over medium heat. Add corn, green onion, and bell pepper. Cook for 6 minutes or until tender. Remove from heat, and set aside.

3. Coat the sides and bottom of a 10-inch cast-iron skillet with vegetable shortening. Place skillet in oven for 5 minutes to melt shortening and heat skillet.

4. In a medium bowl, combine cornmeal mix, flour, sugar, and salt, stirring well. Add reserved vegetables and cheese to cornmeal mixture, stirring to combine.

5. In a separate bowl, combine buttermilk, melted butter, and egg. Add to cornmeal mixture, stirring well. Spoon batter into hot skillet. Bake for 35 to 40 minutes or until firm and golden brown. Cool in pan for 5 minutes.

Baked Boston Brown Bread

Makes 1 loaf

½	cup plus 1 tablespoon yellow cornmeal, divided
1	cup whole-wheat flour
1	cup rye flour
1	cup bread flour
¼	cup firmly packed dark brown sugar
1	teaspoon baking powder
1	teaspoon baking soda
1	teaspoon salt
2	cups whole buttermilk
¾	cup molasses
1	large egg

1. Preheat oven to 350°. Grease a 9x5-inch loaf pan; sprinkle bottom and sides with 1 tablespoon cornmeal; set aside.

2. In a large bowl, combine whole-wheat flour, rye flour, bread flour, remaining ½ cup cornmeal, brown sugar, baking powder, baking soda, and salt.

3. In a separate bowl, combine buttermilk, molasses, and egg, whisking well. Add to flour mixture, stirring until just combined. Spoon batter into prepared pan. Bake for

1 hour and 5 minutes to 1 hour and 10 minutes or until a wooden pick inserted into center comes out clean. Loosely cover with aluminum foil during last 30 minutes to prevent excessive browning.

GRILLED GROUPER WITH HEIRLOOM TOMATO TAPENADE, PAGE 172

3
Savory
ENTRÉES

As the true focal point of the dining experience, the main dish offers inspiration for the entire menu. Certain pairings are classics—a savory breakfast casserole with a refreshing fruit salad or saucy barbecue ribs with baked beans—but mixing and matching dishes can give the home chef quite a repertoire of meals with which to delight her family and friends.

Stuffed Turkey Tenderloins with Fresh Herb Sauce

Makes 12 servings

Stuffed tenderloins:

½	cup plus 2 tablespoons butter, divided
2	cups chopped onion
1	cup chopped celery
2	cloves garlic, minced
1½	teaspoons salt, divided
¾	teaspoon ground black pepper, divided
2	cups crumbled cornbread
1	cup herb-flavored stuffing mix
1	cup dried cranberries
¼	cup chicken broth
4	teaspoons chopped fresh thyme, divided
4	teaspoons chopped fresh rosemary, divided
2	teaspoons poultry seasoning
1	large egg, lightly beaten
6	turkey tenderloins (about 3 pounds)
1	cup all-purpose flour
½	cup olive oil

Sauce:

2	tablespoons butter
2	tablespoons minced shallot
1	tablespoon minced garlic
¼	teaspoon salt
¼	teaspoon ground black pepper
4	teaspoons all-purpose flour
1	tablespoon chopped fresh rosemary
1	tablespoon chopped fresh thyme
2	cups chicken broth
¼	cup heavy whipping cream

Garnish: fresh rosemary sprigs, fresh parsley sprigs, fresh thyme sprigs, fresh cranberries

1. To prepare stuffed tenderloins: In a large skillet, melt ½ cup butter over medium heat. Add onion, celery, garlic, ½ teaspoon salt, and ¼ teaspoon pepper. Cook for 5 to 6 minutes or until tender.

2. In a medium bowl, combine cornbread, stuffing mix, onion mixture, cranberries, chicken broth, 2 teaspoons thyme, 2 teaspoons rosemary, poultry seasoning, and egg, stirring well; set aside.

3. Preheat oven to 350°. Generously grease a 13x9-inch baking dish with remaining 2 tablespoons butter; set aside.

4. Place tenderloins on a clean surface; cut in half lengthwise. Place a piece of heavy-duty plastic wrap on top of tenderloins. Using a meat mallet, flatten to ¼-inch thickness. Season prepared tenderloins on both sides with remaining 1 teaspoon salt and remaining ½ teaspoon pepper. Spoon about ¼ cup stuffing on center of each prepared tenderloin. Roll up tenderloins tightly to enclose stuffing, and secure with wooden picks.

5. In a shallow dish, combine flour, remaining 2 teaspoons thyme, and remaining 2 teaspoons rosemary. Gently coat stuffed tenderloins with flour mixture, shaking off excess.

6. In a large nonstick skillet, heat oil over medium-high heat. Brown tenderloins for 2 minutes on each side. Place in prepared baking dish. Bake for 20 minutes or until a meat thermometer inserted in center of tenderloins registers 165°.

7. To prepare sauce: In a medium saucepan, melt butter over medium heat. Add shallot, garlic, salt, and pepper. Cook for 3 minutes, stirring frequently. Add flour, rosemary, and thyme; cook, stirring constantly, for 2 minutes. Gradually add chicken broth, whisking until smooth. Bring to a simmer; cook for 10 minutes, stirring occasionally. Add cream; simmer for 5 minutes, stirring occasionally.

8. Serve stuffed tenderloins with sauce. Garnish with rosemary, parsley, thyme, and cranberries, if desired.

Roasted Turkey with Garlic-Herb Butter

Makes 8 to 10 servings

1	cup butter, room temperature
¼	cup chopped fresh rosemary
¼	cup chopped fresh thyme
2	tablespoons chopped fresh parsley
2	tablespoons chopped fresh garlic
1½	teaspoons salt
1	teaspoon ground black pepper
1	(16- to 18-pound) whole turkey, giblets removed

Garnish: fresh rosemary sprigs, fresh thyme sprigs, fresh parsley sprigs, fresh currants

1. Preheat oven to 325°.

2. In a medium bowl, combine butter, rosemary, thyme, parsley, garlic, salt, and pepper.

3. Place turkey, breast side up, on a rack in a roasting pan. Evenly rub butter mixture over turkey and under skin. Truss legs with butcher's twine. Cover with aluminum foil, and bake for 3 hours. Remove foil, and bake for 1 hour longer or until a meat thermometer inserted into thigh registers 180°, basting occasionally with pan juices. Remove pan from oven, and let rest for 10 minutes. Garnish with rosemary, thyme, parsley, and currants, if desired. To serve, slice turkey, and pour pan juices on top.

Chicken Cordon Bleu

Makes 4 servings

¼	cup olive oil, divided
2	boneless, skinless chicken breasts
3	tablespoons sour cream
2	teaspoons Dijon mustard
1½	teaspoons chopped fresh rosemary
1½	teaspoons chopped fresh thyme
¼	teaspoon ground black pepper
¼	cup chopped prosciutto
4	ounces sliced Brie
1	cup all-purpose flour
1	large egg, lightly beaten
1	tablespoon water
1	cup panko (Japanese breadcrumbs)

Garnish: fresh thyme

1. Preheat oven to 350°. Pour 2 tablespoons olive oil into an 8x8-inch baking pan; set aside.

2. Cut each chicken breast in half lengthwise. Place each half of chicken breast between 2 sheets of plastic wrap; pound with a meat mallet to ¼-inch thickness.

3. In a small bowl, combine sour cream, mustard, rosemary, thyme, and pepper. Spread one side of each piece of chicken with sour cream mixture, leaving a ¼-inch border. Evenly sprinkle chopped prosciutto on top of sour cream mixture; place Brie on top of prosciutto in center of each piece of chicken. Roll up chicken to enclose prosciutto and Brie. Secure with wooden picks.

4. Place flour in a shallow dish. In a separate shallow dish, whisk together egg and water. In another shallow dish, combine panko and remaining 2 tablespoons olive oil. Coat chicken rolls in flour, shaking off excess. Dip floured chicken rolls in egg mixture, allowing excess to drip off; coat completely with panko mixture.

5. Place pan in oven for 1 to 2 minutes, until oil gets hot. Place chicken rolls, seam side down, in hot pan. Bake, uncovered, for 35 minutes or until a meat thermometer registers 165°. To serve, remove wooden picks. Garnish with fresh thyme, if desired.

Tasso and Andouille Breakfast Casserole

Makes 10 to 12 servings

3   cups frozen country-style hash browns, thawed
1½   cups grated Cheddar cheese, divided
1½   cups grated Swiss cheese, divided
1   cup chopped tasso ham
1   cup chopped andouille sausage
½   cup chopped red bell pepper
½   cup chopped green bell pepper
½   cup chopped green onion
2   cups milk
1   cup baking mix
½   cup sour cream
5   large eggs
1   teaspoon salt
½   teaspoon ground black pepper

1. Lightly grease a 13x9-inch baking dish.

2. In a medium bowl, combine hash browns, 1 cup Cheddar cheese, 1 cup Swiss cheese, ham, sausage, red bell pepper, green bell pepper, and green onion. Spoon hash brown mixture evenly into prepared baking dish.

3. In a separate bowl, combine milk, baking mix, sour cream, eggs, salt, and pepper; whisk until blended. Pour milk mixture evenly over hash brown mixture in baking dish. Sprinkle with remaining ½ cup Cheddar cheese and remaining ½ cup Swiss cheese. Cover and refrigerate for 4 hours to overnight.

4. When ready to bake, let casserole come to room temperature. Preheat oven to 350°.

5. Uncover casserole, and bake for 40 to 45 minutes or until golden brown around the edges and middle is set. Let stand for 10 to 15 minutes before serving.

Ham and Potato au Gratin

Makes 8 to 10 servings

4   tablespoons butter, divided
2   tablespoons all-purpose flour
2   cups hot milk
½   teaspoon dry mustard
1   teaspoon Worcestershire sauce
2   cups grated sharp Cheddar cheese
½   cup chopped onion
¼   cup chopped celery
¼   cup chopped red bell pepper
4   cups thinly sliced Yukon gold potatoes
4   cups chopped cooked ham

1. In a large saucepan, melt 2 tablespoons butter over medium heat. Add flour, and cook for 1 minute, whisking constantly. Gradually whisk in milk. Bring to a simmer, stirring constantly. Cook for 2 to 3 minutes or until mixture thickens. Remove from heat, and add mustard and Worcestershire sauce. Add cheese, stirring until melted and smooth.

2. In a medium sauté pan, melt remaining 2 tablespoons butter over medium heat. Add onion, celery, and red bell pepper; cook for 5 to 6 minutes or until tender.

3. Preheat oven to 350°. Grease a 13x9-inch baking dish. Spoon one-third of cheese mixture evenly over bottom of prepared baking dish. Layer one-half of potatoes over cheese mixture. Spoon one-half of vegetable mixture over potatoes; top with one-half of ham. Repeat layers. Top with remaining one-third of cheese mixture. Cover with aluminum foil, and bake for 45 minutes. Remove foil, and bake for 30 to 40 minutes longer or until potatoes are tender.

Ham, Mushroom, and Spinach Strata

Makes 10 to 12 servings

2 tablespoons olive oil

1 cup chopped yellow onion

1 tablespoon minced garlic

1 (8-ounce) package sliced baby bella mushrooms

1 teaspoon salt, divided

½ teaspoon ground black pepper, divided

6 large eggs

1 cup half-and-half

½ cup sour cream

8 to 10 slices sourdough bread

1 (8-ounce) package cream cheese, softened

2 cups shredded Monterey Jack cheese, divided

½ pound thinly sliced smoked ham

1 (10-ounce) package frozen chopped spinach, thawed and squeezed dry

1. Line a 9-inch square springform pan with heavy-duty aluminum foil. Spray foil with nonstick cooking spray; set aside.

2. In a large skillet, heat olive oil over medium heat. Add onion and garlic; cook for 3 minutes, stirring frequently. Add mushrooms, ½ teaspoon salt, and ¼ teaspoon pepper; cook for 8 minutes, stirring frequently. Set aside to cool.

3. In a medium bowl, whisk together eggs, half-and half, sour cream, remaining ½ teaspoon salt, and remaining ¼ teaspoon pepper.

4. Arrange half of bread slices in bottom of prepared springform pan. Spread with half of cream cheese, and top with ¾ cup Monterey Jack cheese, half of ham, half of spinach, and half of mushroom mixture. Slowly pour half of egg mixture over strata. Repeat layers once, ending with egg mixture. Top with remaining ½ cup Monterey Jack cheese. Cover and refrigerate for at least 1 hour or up to overnight.

5. When ready to bake, let strata come to room temperature. Preheat oven to 350°. Uncover strata, and bake for 1 hour to 1 hour 5 minutes or until browned and set. Let stand for 15 minutes before serving.

Dad's Barbecue Ribs

Makes 10 to 12 servings

2   tablespoons butter
¼   cup finely chopped onion
1½   cups water
1   cup ketchup
⅔   cup white vinegar
3   tablespoons dark brown sugar
2   tablespoons paprika
2   teaspoons ground black pepper
1½   teaspoons Worcestershire sauce
1   teaspoon salt
½   teaspoon ground red pepper
3½   pounds bone-in pork loin country-style ribs (about 16 ribs)

1. In a medium saucepan, melt butter over medium heat. Add onion; cook for 2 minutes, stirring constantly. Add water, ketchup, vinegar, brown sugar, paprika, pepper, Worcestershire sauce, salt, and red pepper, whisking to combine well. Reduce heat to low; simmer for 10 minutes.

2. Grill ribs, covered with grill lid, over medium coals (300° to 350°) for 10 minutes on each side. Dip each rib in sauce; return to grill, and cook, covered with grill lid, for 3 minutes. Repeat procedure three more times, turning ribs over each time.

3. Preheat oven to 325°. Transfer ribs to an aluminum foil roasting pan. Pour remaining sauce over ribs in pan. Cover with aluminum foil. Bake for 1½ hours.

Beef Wellington with Cognac Sauce

Makes 8 servings

Beef Wellington:
1 (2½- to 3-pound) beef tenderloin, trimmed and chain removed
1 teaspoon salt, divided
½ teaspoon ground black pepper, divided
6 tablespoons olive oil, divided
¼ cup minced shallot
¼ cup minced green onion
1 tablespoon minced garlic
1½ cups finely chopped baby bella mushrooms
1½ cups finely chopped shiitake mushrooms
¼ cup chopped fresh parsley
¼ cup chopped fresh sage
¼ cup dry sherry
¼ cup heavy whipping cream
1 (17.3-ounce) package frozen puff pastry sheets, thawed
1 large egg, lightly beaten

Sauce:
2 tablespoons butter
2 tablespoons minced shallot
2 tablespoons minced garlic
¼ teaspoon salt
¼ teaspoon ground black pepper
1 tablespoon all-purpose flour
2 cups beef broth
¼ cup cognac
¼ cup heavy whipping cream

1. To prepare beef Wellington: Preheat oven to 350°. Line a baking sheet with nonstick aluminum foil; set aside.

2. Cut off ends of beef tenderloin so that it is shaped evenly and measures about 10 inches in length; reserve trimmings for another use. Season tenderloin with ½ teaspoon salt and ¼ teaspoon pepper.

3. In a large, heavy skillet, heat 3 tablespoons olive oil over medium-high heat. Sear tenderloin for 7 to 8 minutes, turning frequently, until browned on all sides. Remove from pan, and set aside.

4. In same skillet, heat remaining 3 tablespoons olive oil over medium heat. Add shallot, green onion, and garlic; cook for 2 minutes. Add mushrooms, parsley, sage, sherry, cream, remaining ½ teaspoon salt, and remaining ¼ teaspoon pepper. Cook for 5 to 6 minutes, stirring frequently, until all liquid is absorbed. Remove from heat, and cool slightly.

5. On a lightly floured surface, unfold pastry sheets. Roll each sheet to a 14x10-inch rectangle. Spread mushroom mixture down the center third of one pastry sheet. Place tenderloin on top of mushroom mixture. Top with second pastry sheet, sealing edges to enclose tenderloin completely. Trim edges of pastry, leaving a ½-inch border. Using a fork, crimp edges of pastry to seal.

6. Carefully place beef Wellington on prepared baking sheet. Using a pastry brush, brush outside with egg; decorate, if desired (see Festive Touch below). Bake for 40 to 45 minutes or until pastry is golden brown. Let rest for 5 minutes.

7. To prepare sauce: In a medium saucepan, melt butter over medium heat. Add shallot, garlic, salt, and pepper. Cook for 5 to 6 minutes, stirring frequently. Stir in flour; cook, stirring constantly, for 1 minute. Gradually add broth and cognac, whisking until smooth. Bring to a simmer; reduce heat to low, and cook for 10 minutes, stirring occasionally. Add cream; simmer for 10 minutes, stirring occasionally, until slightly thickened. Serve sauce with beef Wellington.

Festive Touch

To duplicate the poinsettia decoration atop beef Wellington, use a leaf-shaped cookie cutter and a small round tip to cut out shapes from puff pastry trimmings. Using the beaten egg, adhere shapes to the top of the beef Wellington, and brush decoration with egg to achieve even browning during baking.

Cheesy Spaghetti Casserole

Makes 12 servings

2 tablespoons butter
1 cup chopped onion
1 cup chopped green bell pepper
2 pounds ground beef, browned and drained
1 (28-ounce) can diced tomatoes
2 (10-ounce) cans diced tomatoes with green chiles
2 (4-ounce) jars sliced mushrooms, drained
2 (2.25-ounce) cans sliced black olives, drained
1 tablespoon dried oregano
½ teaspoon garlic salt
1 (10-ounce) package thin spaghetti, cooked and kept warm
2 cups grated Cheddar cheese
2 (10.75-ounce) cans cream of mushroom soup
½ cup water
½ cup grated Parmesan cheese

1. Preheat oven to 350°. Grease a 13x9-inch baking dish; set aside.

2. In a Dutch oven, melt butter over medium heat. Add onion and green bell pepper; cook for 5 to 6 minutes or until tender. Add cooked ground beef, tomatoes, mushrooms, olives, oregano, and garlic salt. Bring to a simmer, and cook for 10 minutes.

3. Arrange half of spaghetti evenly in bottom of prepared dish. Spoon half of beef mixture over spaghetti. Sprinkle with 1 cup Cheddar cheese. Repeat layers.

4. In a small bowl, combine soup and water, mixing until smooth. Pour soup mixture over casserole. Top with Parmesan cheese. Bake for 35 to 40 minutes or until hot and bubbly.

Grilled Grouper with Heirloom Tomato Tapenade

Makes 4 servings, pictured on page 160

3 large heirloom tomatoes, seeded and chopped
1 shallot, minced
½ cup finely chopped fennel
1 tablespoon chopped capers
1 tablespoon fresh lemon juice
1 teaspoon chopped fresh thyme
½ teaspoon minced garlic
½ teaspoon salt, divided
½ teaspoon ground black pepper, divided
4 (8-ounce) grouper fillets
1 tablespoon olive oil
Garnish: fennel fronds
(see note for information)

1. In a medium bowl, combine tomato, shallot, fennel, capers, lemon juice, thyme, garlic, ¼ teaspoon salt, and ¼ teaspoon pepper; cover and set aside.

2. Coat grill rack with nonstick nonflammable cooking spray; place on grill over medium-hot coals (350° to 400°). Brush grouper with olive oil, and season with remaining ¼ teaspoon salt and remaining ¼ teaspoon pepper. Place grouper on grill. Cook, covered with grill lid, for 5 to 6 minutes on each side or until fish flakes easily when tested with a fork. Transfer fillets to a plate; spoon tomato mixture over fillets. Garnish with fennel fronds, if desired.

Note: The flavor of fennel fronds—the wispy greens atop fennel stalks—is similar to that of anise and serves as a nice complement to fish dishes, as well as green salads and roasted potatoes.

CHEESY SPAGHETTI CASSEROLE

FRESH STRAWBERRY SOUP, PAGE 186

4

Delicious SALADS AND SOUPS

In this busy day and age when time is a precious commodity, it's especially advantageous to have a go-to cache of tried-and-true dishes that are easy and nutritious. From dressing-drizzled greens and crisp veggie side salads to soul-warming soups and stews, these recipes deliver delicious meals with minimum effort—and maximum enjoyment.

Cucumber and Dill Salad

Makes 6 servings

2　large cucumbers, thinly sliced
2　tablespoons chopped fresh dill
¼　cup apple cider vinegar
1　tablespoon sugar

1. In a medium bowl, combine cucumbers and dill.

2. In a small bowl, whisk together vinegar and sugar until sugar dissolves. Pour over cucumbers, tossing gently to coat.

Arugula Salad with Avocado-Basil Dressing

Makes 6 servings

4　cups washed and torn green leaf lettuce
4　cups arugula
2　cups shredded radicchio
1　cup sliced radishes
2　carrots, grated
Avocado-Basil Dressing (recipe follows)

1. In a large bowl, combine lettuce, arugula, radicchio, radishes, and carrot. Divide evenly among six salad plates. Drizzle with Avocado-Basil Dressing just before serving.

AVOCADO-BASIL DRESSING
Makes about 4 cups

3　medium-size ripe avocados, peeled and seeded
1　small shallot, chopped
2½　cups whole buttermilk
¼　cup sour cream
3　tablespoons chopped fresh basil
2　tablespoons fresh lemon juice
2　tablespoons olive oil
2　tablespoons sugar
2½　teaspoons minced garlic
1½　teaspoons salt
½　teaspoon garlic salt
½　teaspoon ground black pepper

1. In the work bowl of a food processor, combine all ingredients; process until smooth. Cover and chill. Store dressing in an airtight container for up to 1 week.

Watermelon Salad with Watermelon Vinaigrette

Makes 4 servings

Vinaigrette:
1   cup fresh watermelon juice
    (about 2 cups seeded and diced
    watermelon, pureed and strained)
3   tablespoons balsamic vinegar
½   teaspoon salt
¼   teaspoon ground black pepper
¾   cup extra-light olive oil

Salad:
1   (6-ounce) bag baby spinach leaves,
    stems removed
4   cups seeded and diced watermelon
2   ripe avocados, diced
½   cup thinly sliced red onion
¼   cup crumbled feta cheese
Garnish: toasted pine nuts

1. To prepare vinaigrette: In the container
of an electric blender, combine juice,
vinegar, salt, and pepper; process until
blended. With blender running, add oil in a
slow, steady stream; process until blended.
Cover and chill.

2. To prepare salad: Divide spinach,
watermelon, avocado, red onion, and
cheese evenly among four salad plates.
Drizzle with Watermelon Vinaigrette just
before serving. Garnish with toasted pine
nuts, if desired.

Tomato and Basil Salad

Makes 6 servings

2   cups cherry tomatoes, halved
2   cups yellow teardrop tomatoes,
    halved
½   cup chopped fresh basil
2   tablespoons chopped fresh parsley
½   cup olive oil
¼   cup white vinegar
¼   teaspoon salt
¼   teaspoon ground black pepper

1. In a medium bowl, combine tomatoes, basil, and parsley.

2. In a small bowl, whisk together oil, vinegar, salt, and pepper; pour over
tomatoes, tossing gently to combine.

179

BLT Chicken Salad Stuffed Tomatoes

Makes about 2¹/₂ dozen

2   cups chopped cooked chicken
8   slices bacon, cooked and crumbled
¾   cup mayonnaise
⅓   cup finely chopped celery
2   tablespoons finely chopped green onion
½   teaspoon ground black pepper, divided
2   (1-pound) containers small Campari tomatoes (about 30 tomatoes)
¼   teaspoon salt
Garnish: finely shredded green leaf lettuce, crumbled cooked bacon

1. In a medium bowl, combine chicken, bacon, mayonnaise, celery, green onion, and ¼ teaspoon pepper; cover and chill.

2. Using a serrated knife, cut a thin slice off bottom of tomatoes to create a level base. Cut tops from tomatoes. Using a melon baller, remove pulp, leaving shells intact. Turn tomatoes upside down on paper towels to drain for 10 minutes. Season inside of tomato shells with salt and remaining ¼ teaspoon pepper.

3. Spoon chicken salad into each tomato shell. Garnish with lettuce and bacon, if desired.

Crab and Tomato Stacks

Makes 8 servings

Dressing:
¼   cup fresh lime juice
1   tablespoon sugar
1   teaspoon ground cumin
½   teaspoon freshly ground black pepper
¼   teaspoon salt
½   cup vegetable oil

Filling:
2   avocados, diced
¼   cup finely chopped poblano pepper
2   tablespoons chopped fresh cilantro, divided
1   tablespoon finely chopped red onion
⅛   teaspoon salt
1   (8-ounce) container lump crabmeat, picked free of shell

Remaining ingredients:
2   small red tomatoes, sliced ¼ inch thick
2   small orange tomatoes, sliced ¼ inch thick
2   small yellow tomatoes, sliced ¼ inch thick
Garnish: fresh cilantro leaves

1. **To prepare dressing:** In a small bowl, combine lime juice, sugar, cumin, pepper, and salt, whisking until sugar dissolves. Gradually add oil, whisking to combine.

2. **To prepare filling:** In a small bowl, combine avocado, poblano pepper, 1 tablespoon cilantro, red onion, salt, and 2 tablespoons dressing. In a separate small bowl, combine crabmeat, 2 tablespoons dressing, and remaining 1 tablespoon cilantro.

3. **To assemble stacks:** On each serving plate, layer a red tomato slice, avocado mixture, an orange tomato slice, crabmeat mixture, and a yellow tomato slice. Top each with about ½ teaspoon crabmeat mixture. Drizzle with dressing, and garnish with fresh cilantro leaves, if desired.

Fresh Fruit Salad with Basil-Honey Dressing

Makes about 12 cups

½ cup sugar
½ cup water
½ cup fresh basil leaves
1 tablespoon honey
4 cups cantaloupe balls
4 cups honeydew balls
2 cups sliced fresh strawberries
2 cups fresh blueberries
Fresh cantaloupe halves (optional)
Garnish: fresh basil leaves

1. In a small saucepan, combine sugar and water. Bring to a simmer over medium heat, and cook for 10 minutes, stirring frequently.

2. Remove from heat, and add basil leaves; cover and steep for 10 minutes. Remove and discard basil leaves; stir in honey until well combined.

3. Pour honey mixture over fruit, tossing gently to coat. Cover and chill for 2 hours. Serve in cantaloupe halves, and garnish with fresh basil leaves, if desired.

Curried Pineapple Chicken Salad in Pineapple Boats

Makes about 6 cups

4 cups chopped cooked chicken
¾ cup chopped macadamia nuts
½ cup chopped green bell pepper
½ cup chopped celery
⅓ cup chopped green onion
2 tablespoons chopped fresh parsley
1¼ cups mayonnaise
2 teaspoons curry powder
½ teaspoon seasoned salt
¼ teaspoon ground black pepper
1 fresh pineapple
Garnish: sliced green onion

1. In a large bowl, combine chicken, macadamia nuts, bell pepper, celery, green onion, and parsley.

2. In a separate bowl, combine mayonnaise, curry powder, seasoned salt, and pepper. Add mayonnaise mixture to chicken mixture, stirring well to combine. Cover and chill until ready to serve.

3. To serve, slice pineapple into fourths, leaving stem intact. Remove and discard core. Scoop out pulp, leaving shells intact. Chop 1½ cups pineapple, and stir into chicken salad; reserve remaining pineapple for another use.

4. Spoon chicken salad into pineapple shells. Garnish with sliced green onion, if desired.

Mini Taco Salads

Makes 12 servings

2	tablespoons butter, melted
¼	teaspoon garlic salt
2¼	teaspoons ground cumin, divided
4	(10-inch) flour tortillas
¼	cup prepared or commercial salsa
¼	cup sour cream
1	tablespoon chopped fresh cilantro
1	pound ground chuck
¼	cup water
2	teaspoons ancho chili powder
½	teaspoon garlic powder
½	teaspoon paprika
½	teaspoon salt
¼	teaspoon ground black pepper
¼	teaspoon ground red pepper
1	cup finely shredded green leaf lettuce
½	cup seeded and chopped tomato
1	ripe avocado, diced
¼	cup finely grated Cheddar cheese

1. Preheat oven to 325°.

2. In a small bowl, combine melted butter, garlic salt, and ¼ teaspoon cumin; set aside. Using a 4-inch round cutter, cut 3 circles from each tortilla. Brush both sides of tortilla circles with butter mixture. Fit tortilla circles into wells of a 12-cup muffin pan to form cups. Bake for 18 to 20 minutes or until lightly browned and crisp. Cool in pan for 10 minutes; remove to a wire rack, and cool completely.

3. In a small bowl, combine salsa, sour cream, and cilantro. Cover; refrigerate.

4. In a medium skillet over medium-high heat, cook ground chuck for 6 minutes or until browned and crumbly. Drain meat completely. Return to heat; add water, chili powder, remaining 2 teaspoons cumin, garlic powder, paprika, salt, black pepper, and red pepper, stirring well. Spoon meat mixture into prepared tortilla cups. Top with lettuce, salsa mixture, tomato, avocado, and cheese. Serve immediately.

Easy Corn Salad

Makes 6 to 8 servings

4	cups fresh corn kernels or 1 (16-ounce) package frozen corn, thawed
1	cup chopped green bell pepper
1	cup chopped red bell pepper
½	cup heavy whipping cream
2	tablespoons butter
¼	teaspoon salt
¼	teaspoon ground black pepper

1. In a medium saucepan, cook fresh corn in boiling water to cover for 6 to 8 minutes or until tender; drain. If using frozen corn, cook according to package directions.

2. Place cooked corn in a medium skillet. Add remaining ingredients, and cook over medium heat until vegetables are tender. Serve warm or chilled.

Gazpacho

Makes 6 to 8 servings

3   cups spicy vegetable juice
3   plum tomatoes, chopped
1   cup chopped red bell pepper
1   cup chopped green bell pepper
½   cup seeded and chopped cucumber
½   cup chopped red onion
½   cup chopped fresh cilantro
1   teaspoon minced garlic
1   tablespoon lemon juice
1   tablespoon Worcestershire sauce
¼   teaspoon hot sauce

1. In the work bowl of a food processor, pour 1 cup vegetable juice. Add one-third each of tomatoes, red bell pepper, green bell pepper, cucumber, onion, cilantro, and garlic. Process to desired consistency. Repeat procedure twice with remaining vegetable juice and vegetables. Add lemon juice, Worcestershire, and hot sauce. Cover and chill for at least 4 hours.

Fresh Strawberry Soup

Makes 6 servings

2   cups sliced fresh strawberries
1   cup milk
1   cup heavy whipping cream
1   cup sweet white wine
½   cup sugar
½   cup sour cream
½   cup honey
Garnish: whipped cream

1. In the container of an electric blender or food processor, combine all ingredients (except garnish). Process until smooth, stopping to scrape down sides of container as needed. Transfer to an airtight container, and chill.

2. To serve, stir well, and garnish with whipped cream, if desired.

Chicken, Mushroom, and Wild Rice Stew
Makes about 3 quarts

¼ cup butter
2 tablespoons olive oil
2 cups chopped onion
1 cup chopped celery
1 tablespoon minced garlic
2 (8-ounce) containers sliced baby bella mushrooms
6 tablespoons all-purpose flour
2 teaspoons garlic powder
1 teaspoon salt
1 teaspoon ground white pepper
½ teaspoon ground black pepper
2 quarts chicken broth
4 cups chopped cooked chicken
3 cups cooked wild rice
1 cup heavy whipping cream
2 tablespoons chopped fresh thyme
2 tablespoons dry sherry
Garnish: fresh thyme

1. In a large Dutch oven, melt butter with olive oil over medium heat. Add onion and celery, and cook for 5 minutes. Add garlic, and cook for 2 minutes. Add mushrooms, and cook for 10 minutes, stirring frequently. Add flour, garlic powder, salt, white pepper, and black pepper; cook for 2 minutes, stirring constantly.

2. Gradually add chicken broth, stirring until smooth. Bring to a simmer; add chicken and rice, and cook for 20 minutes, stirring occasionally. Add cream and thyme; return to a simmer, and cook for 10 minutes. Stir in sherry. Garnish with thyme, if desired.

Corn Chowder

Makes about 4½ quarts

¼	cup butter
4	cups diced onion
1	cup diced green bell pepper
1	cup diced red bell pepper
½	cup all-purpose flour
2	quarts chicken broth
6	cups diced potatoes
1	cup crushed oyster crackers
2	teaspoons salt
1	teaspoon ground black pepper
¼	teaspoon ground red pepper
1	quart half-and-half
5	cups fresh or frozen corn kernels

Garnish: chopped red bell pepper, chopped yellow bell pepper, chopped fresh parsley

1. In a large Dutch oven, melt butter over medium-high heat. Add onion and bell pepper; cook for 10 minutes, stirring frequently. Add flour, and cook for 1 minute, stirring constantly. Gradually whisk in chicken broth; bring to a boil. Add potatoes, and cook for 10 to 15 minutes or until potatoes are tender.

2. Add crushed crackers, salt, black pepper, and red pepper, stirring well. Reduce heat to medium-low. Add half-and-half and corn. Bring to a simmer, and cook for 40 to 50 minutes or until slightly thickened. Garnish with bell pepper and parsley, if desired.

Roasted Sweet Potato Bisque

Makes 10 to 12 servings

8	cups diced sweet potatoes
4	tablespoons olive oil, divided
2	tablespoons butter
1	cup finely chopped onion
2	teaspoons minced garlic
2	tablespoons all-purpose flour
2	quarts chicken broth
1	teaspoon curry powder
1	teaspoon salt
½	teaspoon ground white pepper
1	cup heavy whipping cream
1	cup sour cream

Garnish: crumbled cooked bacon

1. Preheat oven to 450°. Line a baking sheet with aluminum foil; set aside.

2. In a large bowl, combine sweet potatoes and 2 tablespoons olive oil; toss to coat evenly. Spread potatoes in an even layer on prepared baking sheet. Bake for 45 minutes, stirring halfway through.

3. In a large Dutch oven, melt butter with remaining 2 tablespoons olive oil over medium heat. Add onion and garlic; cook for 3 minutes, stirring frequently, until tender. Add roasted sweet potatoes, stirring to combine. Add flour; cook, stirring constantly, for 2 minutes. Add chicken broth, curry powder, salt, and white pepper; cook for 10 minutes. Remove from heat, and cool slightly.

4. In the work bowl of a food processor, puree mixture in batches until smooth. Return mixture to Dutch oven. Add cream and sour cream, whisking until smooth; simmer over medium-low heat for 10 minutes. Garnish with bacon, if desired.

Vermont Cheddar Cheese Soup

Makes about 2 quarts

¼	cup butter
1	cup chopped yellow onion
½	cup chopped carrot
½	cup chopped celery
1	tablespoon minced garlic
1	cup dry white wine
⅓	cup all-purpose flour
1	quart chicken broth
2	cups heavy whipping cream
2	tablespoons fresh lemon juice
4½	teaspoons sugar
1	teaspoon paprika
1	teaspoon ground mustard
¾	teaspoon salt
½	teaspoon garlic powder
½	teaspoon ground red pepper
½	teaspoon ground black pepper
24	ounces Vermont Cheddar cheese, grated

Garnish: pumpernickel croutons,
grated Vermont Cheddar cheese

1. In a Dutch oven, melt butter over medium heat. Add onion, carrot, celery, and garlic; cook for 10 minutes, stirring occasionally, until tender. Add wine; cook for 8 to 10 minutes, stirring occasionally, until liquid is almost evaporated. Add flour; cook for 3 minutes, stirring constantly. Gradually add chicken broth, stirring constantly, until smooth. Add cream, lemon juice, sugar, paprika, ground mustard, salt, garlic powder, red pepper, and black pepper. Bring to a simmer. Reduce heat to low. Add cheese, stirring until cheese is melted. Garnish with pumpernickel croutons and grated cheese, if desired.

Mulligan Stew

Makes about 6 quarts

2	pounds (1-inch cube) beef tips
2	pounds lamb, cut into 1-inch pieces
2½	teaspoons salt, divided
1½	teaspoons ground black pepper, divided
½	cup all-purpose flour
6	tablespoons olive oil, divided
2	medium-size yellow onions, cut into 1-inch pieces
1	(8-ounce) package sliced baby bella mushrooms
1	tablespoon minced garlic
1	cup red wine
6	cups beef broth
3	(14.5-ounce) cans fire-roasted diced tomatoes
1	(6-ounce) can tomato paste
6	medium carrots, cut into 1-inch slices
4	ribs celery, cut into ½-inch slices
1	tablespoon sugar
4	cups cubed potatoes
3	tablespoons chopped fresh thyme

Garnish: fresh thyme sprigs

1. In a large bowl, combine beef, lamb, 1 teaspoon salt, and ½ teaspoon pepper. Add flour, tossing gently to coat.

2. In a large Dutch oven, heat 4 tablespoons olive oil over medium heat. Add meat, and cook for 10 to 12 minutes, stirring frequently, until browned. Remove meat from Dutch oven; set aside.

3. To Dutch oven, add remaining 2 tablespoons olive oil, onion, mushrooms, and garlic; cook for 4 minutes, stirring frequently. Add wine; cook for 2 minutes. Add broth, tomatoes, tomato paste, carrot, celery, sugar, remaining 1½ teaspoons salt, remaining 1 teaspoon pepper, and browned meat. Bring to a boil; reduce heat to medium-low, and simmer, uncovered, for 1½ hours, stirring occasionally. Add potatoes; cook for 12 to 15 minutes or until potatoes are fork-tender. Add thyme, stirring well. Garnish with fresh thyme sprigs, if desired.

Lobster Bisque

Makes about 2 quarts

½ cup plus 2 tablespoons butter, divided
2 tablespoons olive oil
4 (8- to 10-ounce) lobster tails
1½ cups chopped yellow onion
¾ cup chopped carrot
¾ cup chopped celery
2 teaspoons salt
¾ teaspoon ground black pepper
1 cup dry sherry
3 tablespoons tomato paste
1 tablespoon minced garlic
2 quarts water
6 bay leaves
½ cup all-purpose flour
1½ cups heavy whipping cream
Garnish: sliced fresh chives

1. In a large Dutch oven, melt 2 tablespoons butter with olive oil over medium-high heat. Add lobster tails, onion, carrot, celery, salt, and pepper, stirring to combine. Cover and cook for 6 to 8 minutes, stirring occasionally, or until vegetables are tender and lobster shells are red. Remove from heat. Remove lobster tails from Dutch oven. Remove meat from lobster tails, and set aside, reserving shells.

2. Return Dutch oven to heat. Add sherry; cook for 2 minutes. Add tomato paste and garlic; cook for 2 to 3 minutes, stirring frequently. Add water, bay leaves, and reserved lobster shells; bring to a boil. Reduce heat to medium-low, and simmer, covered, for 45 minutes. Strain lobster broth, discarding solids; set aside.

3. In a Dutch oven, melt remaining ½ cup butter over medium heat. Add flour, and cook for 3 minutes, stirring constantly. Gradually add lobster broth, whisking until smooth. Bring to a boil; reduce heat to medium-low, and simmer for 20 minutes. Add cream, whisking until smooth; cook for 3 to 4 minutes or until heated through. Top servings with lobster meat, and garnish with chives, if desired.

Seafood Chowder

Makes about 4½ quarts

½ pound bacon, diced
2 cups chopped yellow onion
1 cup chopped celery
1 cup chopped carrot
1 tablespoon minced garlic
6 bay leaves
2 teaspoons salt
1 teaspoon ground black pepper
½ cup all-purpose flour
6 cups seafood stock*
2 pounds potatoes, cut into 1-inch pieces
2 cups fresh or frozen corn kernels
2 cups heavy whipping cream
1 pound fresh cod fillets, cut into 1-inch pieces
1 pound medium fresh shrimp, peeled and deveined
1 pound large fresh sea scallops, cut into 1-inch pieces
1 (8-ounce) container lump crabmeat, picked free of shell

1. In a large Dutch oven, cook bacon over medium heat until crispy. Add onion, celery, carrot, garlic, bay leaves, salt, and pepper. Cook for 4 to 5 minutes, stirring occasionally, until tender. Add flour; cook for 3 minutes, stirring constantly. Add seafood stock, stirring until smooth. Add potatoes and corn. Bring to a boil, reduce heat to medium-low, and simmer for 10 to 12 minutes or until potatoes are fork-tender. Add cream, and return to a simmer. Add cod, shrimp, scallops, and crabmeat; simmer for 3 to 5 minutes or until seafood reaches desired degree of doneness. Remove bay leaves, and discard. Serve with oyster crackers.

*Seafood stock is available at Whole Foods and other specialty markets.

BROCCOLI FETTUCCINE AU GRATIN, PAGE 202

5

Delectable
SIDE DISHES

Much more than just the supporting cast for the entrée, side dishes shine in a light all their own. Oven-roasted herbed potato wedges alongside prime rib, gravy-drenched cornbread dressing next to the Thanksgiving turkey—these savory sides offer their own delectable contributions to the success of the meal.

Pole Beans with Pancetta

Makes 10 to 12 servings

6	quarts water
1	tablespoon plus 1¾ teaspoons salt, divided
4	pounds pole beans, stemmed and snapped
2	tablespoons olive oil
1	(5-ounce) package pancetta, chopped
½	cup minced shallots
2	teaspoons minced garlic
3	cups chicken broth
1	tablespoon sugar
½	teaspoon ground black pepper

1. In a large Dutch oven, bring water and 1 tablespoon salt to a boil. Add beans, return to a boil, and cook for 10 minutes. Drain beans, and set aside.

2. In Dutch oven, heat olive oil over medium heat. Add pancetta; cook for 2 to 3 minutes. Add shallot and garlic; cook for 2 minutes, stirring frequently. Add beans, chicken broth, sugar, remaining 1¾ teaspoons salt, and pepper. Bring to a simmer; cook, uncovered, for 45 minutes, stirring frequently.

Southern-Style Baked Beans

Makes 12 servings

6	slices thick-sliced bacon
1½	cups chopped onion
2	teaspoons minced garlic
2	(28-ounce) cans pork and beans, drained
⅓	cup firmly packed dark brown sugar
1	tablespoon teriyaki sauce
1	tablespoon spicy brown mustard
½	teaspoon salt
½	teaspoon ground black pepper

1. In a large skillet, cook bacon over medium heat until crisp. Crumble bacon, and set aside. Pour bacon drippings into a small bowl, reserving 2 tablespoons drippings in skillet. Add onion and garlic to skillet; cook over medium heat, stirring frequently, for 3 to 4 minutes or until tender.

2. Preheat oven to 350°. In a large bowl, combine pork and beans, remaining reserved drippings, onion mixture, brown sugar, teriyaki sauce, mustard, salt, and pepper.

3. Spoon beans into a 2-quart baking dish. Top with crumbled bacon. Bake, uncovered, for 1 hour 15 minutes or until bubbly.

Fresh Tomato Pie

Makes 1 (9-inch) pie

6	large tomatoes
1	teaspoon salt
1	cup shredded mozzarella cheese
1	cup shredded Cheddar cheese
1	cup mayonnaise
1	(9-inch) deep-dish frozen pie crust, baked according to package directions
1	bunch green onions, sliced
½	cup sliced fresh basil

Garnish: fresh basil

1. Peel and cut tomatoes into ¼-inch-thick slices. Place tomatoes in a colander, and sprinkle with 1 teaspoon salt. Set aside to drain.

2. Preheat oven to 350°.

3. In a medium bowl, combine cheeses and mayonnaise.

4. Place drained tomatoes in baked pie crust. Sprinkle evenly with green onions and basil. Spread mayonnaise mixture over the top. Bake for 30 to 40 minutes or until lightly browned. Garnish with fresh basil, if desired.

Classic Potato Salad

Makes 10 to 12 servings

5	pounds russet potatoes, peeled and diced
6	hard-boiled eggs, peeled and chopped
2	cups chopped yellow onion
1	cup chopped celery
¾	cup sweet pickle relish
1	cup mayonnaise
2	tablespoons prepared mustard
1	teaspoon salt
½	teaspoon ground black pepper

Garnish: fresh parsley, green olives, paprika

1. Place potatoes in a Dutch oven; add enough salted water to cover. Bring to a boil over high heat; boil for 8 to 10 minutes or until tender. Drain and cool.

2. In a large bowl, combine potatoes, eggs, onion, celery, and sweet pickle relish.

3. In a small bowl, combine mayonnaise, mustard, salt, and pepper, stirring well.

4. Add mayonnaise mixture to potato mixture, tossing gently to coat. Cover and chill for 2 hours. Garnish with parsley, green olives, and paprika, if desired.

Red and Gold Potatoes with Herbs

Makes 8 servings

2 pounds red potatoes,
   quartered lengthwise
2 pounds Yukon gold potatoes,
   quartered lengthwise
3 tablespoons olive oil
2 teaspoons minced garlic
2 tablespoons chopped fresh thyme
1 tablespoon chopped fresh rosemary
1 tablespoon chopped fresh parsley
1¼ teaspoons salt
½ teaspoon ground black pepper
Garnish: fresh thyme and rosemary

1. Preheat oven to 400°. Line a large shallow roasting pan with nonstick aluminum foil.

2. In a large bowl, combine potatoes and remaining ingredients (except garnish), tossing gently to coat. Arrange potatoes in a single layer in prepared pan. Bake for 40 to 45 minutes or until potatoes are golden and tender, stirring occasionally. Garnish with fresh thyme and rosemary, if desired.

Herbed Home Fries with Caramelized Onions

Makes 10 to 12 servings

1 (3-pound) bag red potatoes, diced
   into ¾-inch cubes
10 tablespoons butter, divided
2 large yellow onions, sliced
   ⅛ inch thick
1 tablespoon balsamic vinegar
1 teaspoon salt, divided
½ teaspoon ground black pepper,
   divided
1 tablespoon chopped fresh thyme
1 tablespoon chopped fresh parsley
1½ teaspoons chopped fresh rosemary

1. In a Dutch oven, cook potatoes for 3 to 4 minutes in enough boiling salted water to cover. (Potatoes should be crisp-tender.) Drain potatoes, and set aside to cool.

2. In a large nonstick skillet, melt 4 tablespoons butter over medium-high heat. Add onion; cook, stirring frequently, for 15 minutes or until caramelized. Add vinegar, ½ teaspoon salt, and ¼ teaspoon pepper; cook, stirring constantly, until liquid evaporates, about 1 to 2 minutes. Transfer onions to a small bowl.

3. In same skillet, melt remaining 6 tablespoons butter over medium heat. Add

potatoes, pressing down with a spatula. Cook, without stirring, for 7 to 8 minutes or until browned on one side. Turn potatoes over with spatula, press down again, and cook, without stirring, for 7 to 8 minutes or until well browned. Turn potatoes once more, and cook for an additional 7 to 8 minutes or until all potatoes are browned and crispy.

4. Add onions, thyme, parsley, rosemary, remaining ½ teaspoon salt, and remaining ¼ teaspoon pepper to potatoes, stirring to combine. Serve immediately.

Caramelized Vidalia Onion and Potato Gratin

Makes 10 to 12 servings

¼   cup butter
2   large yellow onions, sliced
     ⅛ inch thick
1   tablespoon balsamic vinegar
2   teaspoons salt, divided
¾   teaspoon ground black pepper, divided
1   cup heavy whipping cream
1   cup grated Gruyère cheese
1   cup grated Monterey Jack cheese
3   pounds Yukon gold potatoes,
     peeled and thinly sliced

1. In a large skillet, melt butter over medium-low heat. Add onions; cover and cook for 30 minutes, stirring occasionally. Uncover and increase heat to medium-high. Add vinegar, ½ teaspoon salt, and ¼ teaspoon pepper. Cook for 4 to 5 minutes, stirring constantly, until golden brown. Remove from heat; set aside.

2. Preheat oven to 400°.

3. In a medium bowl, whisk together cream, remaining 1½ teaspoons salt, and remaining ½ teaspoon pepper. In a separate bowl, combine cheeses.

4. In a 2½-quart baking dish, layer half of potatoes, half of onion mixture, half of cheese, and half of cream mixture; repeat layers. Place on a baking sheet. Cover with nonstick aluminum foil. Bake for 1 hour 30 minutes. Remove foil, and bake for 15 minutes longer or until potatoes are tender. Let stand for 15 minutes before serving.

Broccoli Fettuccine au Gratin

Makes 6 servings, pictured on page 194

1   tablespoon butter
8   ounces fettuccine noodles, cooked
3   cups small broccoli florets, blanched
½   cup chopped red bell pepper
1   (8-ounce) package cream cheese,
     softened
1¼   cups grated Parmigiano-Reggiano
     cheese, divided
2   large eggs
1   teaspoon minced garlic
½   teaspoon salt
¼   teaspoon ground black pepper
1   cup heavy whipping cream

1. Preheat oven to 350°. Grease an 8x8-inch baking dish with butter; set aside. In a medium bowl, combine fettuccine, broccoli, and red bell pepper; spoon into prepared dish.

2. In a medium bowl, combine cream cheese, 1 cup cheese, eggs, garlic, salt, and pepper. Beat at medium speed with an electric mixer until combined; stir in cream. Pour cream cheese mixture over fettuccine mixture. Top with remaining ¼ cup cheese. Bake for 30 minutes.

Southern Cornbread Dressing

Makes 10 to 12 servings

2   cups white cornmeal
2   teaspoons baking powder
1   teaspoon baking soda
1   teaspoon salt, divided
5   large eggs, divided
2   cups whole buttermilk
2   tablespoons bacon drippings
⅓   cup butter
2   cups chopped onion
1   cup chopped green onion
1   cup chopped celery
10   slices white bread, crumbled
1   tablespoon poultry seasoning
2   teaspoons dried rubbed sage
     (optional)
1   teaspoon ground black pepper
1   quart chicken broth
1   cup milk

1. Preheat oven to 450°. Lightly grease a 13x9-inch baking dish; set aside.

2. In a large bowl, combine cornmeal, baking powder, baking soda, and ½ teaspoon salt. Add 2 eggs, buttermilk, and bacon drippings, stirring until well combined.

3. Place a well-greased 10-inch cast-iron skillet in oven for 4 minutes or until hot. Spoon batter into hot skillet. Bake for 30 minutes or until golden brown. Cool in pan for 10 minutes. Crumble; set aside.

4. In a large skillet, melt butter over medium-high heat. Add onion, green onion, and celery. Cook, stirring frequently, for 7 to 8 minutes or until tender.

5. In a large bowl, combine crumbled cornbread, crumbled white bread, onion mixture, remaining 3 eggs, poultry seasoning, sage, pepper, and remaining ½ teaspoon salt. Add chicken broth and milk, stirring well. Spoon dressing mixture into prepared baking dish. Bake for 45 to 50 minutes or until lightly browned and set.

Broccoli Casserole

Makes 8 to 10 servings

¼ cup butter
½ cup chopped celery
½ cup chopped onion
1 tablespoon garlic powder
2 tablespoons all-purpose flour
1½ cups milk
2 cups shredded Cheddar cheese
2 (10-ounce) packages frozen chopped broccoli, thawed
1 (10.75-ounce) can cream of mushroom soup
½ teaspoon salt
¼ teaspoon ground black pepper
1 sleeve round buttery crackers, crushed
2 tablespoons butter, melted

1. Preheat oven to 350°. Lightly grease a 2½-quart baking dish; set aside.

2. In a large skillet, melt ¼ cup butter over medium heat. Add celery, onion, and garlic powder; cook for 3 to 4 minutes or until vegetables are tender. Add flour; cook for 2 minutes, stirring constantly. Gradually add milk, stirring until smooth. Add cheese, stirring until cheese is melted. Add broccoli, cream of mushroom soup, salt, and pepper, stirring well; cook for 1 minute. Spoon mixture into prepared baking dish.

3. In a small bowl, combine crackers and melted butter. Sprinkle evenly over broccoli mixture. Bake for 20 to 25 minutes or until browned and bubbly.

Macaroni and Cheese

Makes 10 to 12 servings

4 cups milk
2 cups heavy whipping cream, divided
½ cup butter
1 tablespoon salt
1 (16-ounce) package penne pasta
2 cups freshly grated Parmesan cheese, divided
1 tablespoon chopped fresh parsley
Paprika

1. Preheat oven to 350°. Lightly grease a 13x9-inch baking dish; set aside.

2. In a Dutch oven, combine milk, 1 cup cream, butter, and salt. Bring to a simmer over medium heat. Add pasta; cook for 12 minutes, stirring frequently. Remove from heat; add 1 cup Parmesan cheese, stirring until cheese is melted.

3. Spoon pasta mixture into prepared baking dish. Pour remaining 1 cup cream over pasta. Top with remaining 1 cup Parmesan cheese. Evenly sprinkle parsley and paprika over cheese. Bake for 20 minutes or until lightly browned and bubbly.

Hot Baked Fruit with Granola-Nut Topping

Makes 10 to 12 servings

2	Granny Smith apples, cored and diced
2	Braeburn apples, cored and diced
2	green Anjou pears, cored and diced
1	(5-ounce) package dried cherries
1	cup firmly packed light brown sugar
¼	cup all-purpose flour
1	teaspoon ground cinnamon
6	tablespoons butter, melted
2	cups applesauce
	Granola-Nut Topping (recipe follows)

1. Preheat oven to 350°.

2. In a medium bowl, combine apples, pears, and dried cherries.

3. In a separate bowl, combine brown sugar, flour, and cinnamon. Stir in melted butter. Add applesauce, stirring well. Combine brown sugar mixture and fruit mixture. Spoon into an ungreased 13x9-inch baking dish. Bake for 45 to 50 minutes or until fruit is tender. Top with Granola-Nut Topping.

GRANOLA-NUT TOPPING

Makes about 4½ cups

1	cup old-fashioned oats
½	cup chopped pecans
½	cup slivered almonds
½	cup chopped walnuts
½	cup sweetened flaked coconut
1	teaspoon ground cinnamon
¼	cup butter
3	tablespoons honey
3	tablespoons light brown sugar

1. Preheat oven to 275°. Line a rimmed baking sheet with aluminum foil. Spray foil with nonstick cooking spray; set aside.

2. In a medium bowl, combine oats, pecans, almonds, walnuts, coconut, and cinnamon.

3. In a small saucepan, combine butter, honey, and brown sugar. Bring to a boil over medium heat, stirring until sugar is dissolved. Add butter mixture to oat mixture, stirring well. Spread oat mixture in an even layer on prepared baking sheet. Bake for 35 to 40 minutes or until browned, stirring at 10-minute intervals. Let cool to room temperature. Store in an airtight container.

Tasty Topping

Granola-Nut Topping is a recipe you'll want to keep handy. We found it to be equally tasty sprinkled on yogurt, ice cream, and even pudding—though we must confess that, once it cooled a bit, we simply enjoyed nibbling it by the handful, straight off the baking sheet!

CHOCOLATE-COVERED ALMOND TOFFEE, PAGE 224

6
Heavenly
DESSERTS

Southerners love to finish off a meal with a sugary flourish. From refreshing fruit sorbets and towering cakes to wonderfully rich banana pudding and pecan pie—and every heavenly confection in between— desserts offer a sweet finale to any occasion.

Lemon-Raspberry Pound Cake with Vanilla Buttercream

Makes 1 (8-inch) cake, pictured on cover

Cake:

3	cups sugar
¾	cup butter-flavored shortening
¾	cup unsalted butter, softened
3	tablespoons lemon zest
8	large eggs
3	cups all-purpose flour
1½	teaspoons salt
¾	cup half-and-half
3	teaspoons lemon extract
1½	teaspoons vanilla extract

Raspberry filling:

1	(10-ounce) package frozen raspberries, thawed
1	cup fresh raspberries
½	cup sugar
3	tablespoons cornstarch

Lemon curd:

1	cup sugar
1	tablespoon lemon zest
½	cup fresh lemon juice
2	large eggs
1	egg yolk
½	vanilla bean, split lengthwise and scraped, seeds reserved
⅛	teaspoon salt
¼	cup sour cream
2	tablespoons cornstarch
1	tablespoon unsalted butter, softened

Buttercream:

5	egg whites
1½	cups sugar
1	teaspoon clear vanilla extract
½	vanilla bean, split lengthwise and scraped, seeds reserved
2	cups unsalted butter, softened
½	cup confectioners' sugar

Garnish: lemon slices, raspberries

1. To prepare cake: Preheat oven to 300°. Spray 3 (8-inch) cake pans with nonstick baking spray with flour. Line bottoms of pans with parchment paper, and spray again; set aside.

2. In a medium bowl, beat sugar, shortening, butter, and zest at medium speed with an electric mixer until fluffy. Add eggs, one at a time, beating well after each addition.

3. In a small bowl, sift together flour and salt. Gradually add to butter mixture alternately with half-and-half, beginning and ending with flour mixture, beating just until combined after each addition. Beat in lemon extract and vanilla. Pour batter evenly into prepared pans, smoothing top with an offset spatula.

4. Bake for 55 minutes to 1 hour or until a wooden pick inserted near center comes out clean. Cool cake in pans for 10 minutes; invert onto wire racks, and remove parchment paper. Cool completely.

5. To prepare raspberry filling: In a medium saucepan, combine thawed raspberries, fresh raspberries, and sugar. Cook over medium heat, stirring often, until bubbly. Over a bowl, strain mixture through a fine-mesh sieve, pressing with the back of a spoon; discard solids. Return strained mixture to pan; sift cornstarch over mixture. Cook, stirring constantly, until mixture thickens. Chill mixture for at least 2 hours before using. Store, covered, in refrigerator for up to 3 days.

6. To prepare lemon curd: In a medium heavy saucepan, whisk together sugar, lemon zest, lemon juice, eggs, egg yolk, reserved vanilla bean seeds, and salt. Cook over medium heat, whisking constantly, for 8 to 10 minutes or until mixture thickens. Add sour cream, cornstarch, and butter, stirring until butter melts. Remove from heat. Over a bowl, strain mixture through a fine-mesh strainer, pressing with the back of a spoon; discard solids. Place a piece of plastic wrap directly on surface of curd. Chill for at least 2 hours before using.

7. To prepare buttercream: In the bowl of a heavy-duty stand mixer, combine egg whites, sugar, vanilla extract, and vanilla bean seeds. Place bowl over a pot of simmering water. Whisk constantly until mixture registers 140° on an instant-read candy thermometer, about 3 minutes. Place bowl on stand mixer, and beat at high speed with whip attachment until cooled and glossy, about 15 minutes. Reduce mixer speed to low; add butter, 1 tablespoon at a time, beating well after each addition. Beat in confectioners' sugar. Use immediately, or cover and refrigerate for up to 1 week. If refrigerated, bring to room temperature, and beat until smooth before using.

8. To assemble cake: Spread one cake layer with half of raspberry filling. Spread about 1½ cups buttercream over raspberry layer. Repeat with second cake layer, remaining raspberry filling, and 1½ cups buttercream. Top with third cake layer. Frost sides and top of cake with remaining buttercream. Spread a thin layer of lemon curd over top of cake. Garnish with lemon slices and raspberries, if desired. Store cake, covered, in refrigerator for up to 5 days.

Toffee-Topped Caramel Cake

Makes 1 (9-inch) cake

Cake:
1	cup butter, softened
1	cup sugar
1	cup firmly packed dark brown sugar
1	teaspoon vanilla extract
6	large eggs
2½	cups all-purpose flour
1	teaspoon baking powder
1	teaspoon baking soda
¼	teaspoon salt
1	cup sour cream

Caramel:
2	cups firmly packed light brown sugar
⅔	cup evaporated milk
⅓	cup butter

Frosting:
½	cup firmly packed dark brown sugar
¼	cup heavy whipping cream
½	cup plus 2 tablespoons butter, softened and divided
1	(8-ounce) package cream cheese, softened
½	teaspoon vanilla extract
5	cups confectioners' sugar, sifted

Garnish: chopped English toffee-flavored candy bars

1. To prepare cake: Preheat oven to 350°. Spray 3 (9-inch) round cake pans with nonstick baking spray with flour; set aside.

2. In a large bowl, beat butter, sugar, and brown sugar at medium speed with an electric mixer until fluffy. Add vanilla, beating to combine. Add eggs, one at a time, beating well after each addition.

3. In a medium bowl, sift together flour, baking powder, baking soda, and salt. Gradually add to butter mixture alternately with sour cream, beginning and ending with flour mixture. Spoon batter into prepared pans. Bake for 15 to 17 minutes or until a wooden pick inserted in center comes out clean. Let cool in pans for 10 minutes. Remove cake from pans, and cool completely on wire racks.

4. To prepare caramel: In a small saucepan, combine brown sugar, evaporated milk, and butter. Cook over medium heat, stirring until sugar is dissolved. Cook, without stirring, until a candy thermometer registers 238°.

5. Transfer caramel mixture to a heat-resistant bowl. Beat at medium speed with an electric mixer for 2 to 3 minutes or until mixture thickens slightly and is easy to spread. Working quickly, spread caramel mixture on top of 2 cake layers. Refrigerate for 15 minutes or until set.

6. To prepare frosting : In a small saucepan, combine brown sugar, cream, and 2 tablespoons butter over medium heat. Cook for 3 to 4 minutes, stirring constantly, until sugar is dissolved. Cool completely.

7. In a large bowl, beat cream cheese and remaining ½ cup butter at medium speed with an electric mixer until smooth. Add brown sugar mixture and vanilla, beating well. Gradually add confectioners' sugar, beating until smooth.

8. To assemble cake: Place one caramel-covered layer on a cake plate. Spread a thin layer of frosting over caramel. Place another caramel-covered layer on top of frosting. Spread a thin layer of frosting over caramel. Top with plain cake layer. Frost top and sides of cake with remaining frosting. Garnish with chopped candy bars, if desired.

Southern Butter Pecan Cake

Makes 1 (9-inch) cake

Cake:

1	cup butter, softened
1	cup sugar
1	cup firmly packed dark brown sugar
1	teaspoon vanilla extract
6	large eggs
2½	cups all-purpose flour
1	teaspoon baking powder
1	teaspoon baking soda
¼	teaspoon salt
1	cup sour cream

Frosting:

½	cup firmly packed dark brown sugar
¼	cup heavy whipping cream
½	cup plus 2 tablespoons butter, softened and divided
1	(8-ounce) package cream cheese, softened
½	teaspoon vanilla extract
5	cups confectioners' sugar, sifted
2	cups toasted chopped pecans

Garnish: 1 (5-ounce) package glazed pecans

1. To prepare cake: Preheat oven to 350°. Grease and flour 3 (9-inch) round cake pans.

2. In a large bowl, beat butter and sugars at medium speed with an electric mixer until fluffy. Add vanilla, beating to combine. Add eggs, one at a time, beating well after each addition.

3. In a medium bowl, sift together flour, baking powder, baking soda, and salt. Gradually add to butter mixture alternately with sour cream, beginning and ending with flour mixture. Spoon batter into prepared pans. Bake for 15 to 17 minutes or until a wooden pick inserted in center comes out clean. Cool in pans for 10 minutes. Remove from pans, and cool completely on wire racks.

4. To prepare frosting: In a small saucepan, combine brown sugar, cream, and 2 tablespoons butter over medium heat. Cook for 3 to 4 minutes, stirring constantly, until sugar is dissolved. Cool completely.

5. In a large bowl, beat cream cheese and remaining ½ cup butter at medium speed with an electric mixer until smooth. Add brown sugar mixture and vanilla, beating until combined. Gradually add confectioners' sugar, beating until smooth. Add pecans, beating well.

6. To assemble cake: Spread frosting between layers and on top and sides of cake. Garnish with glazed pecans, if desired.

Note: The pecans in the frosting tend to pull crumbs off the cake. Try preparing the cake layers a day or two ahead and freezing them, tightly wrapped in plastic wrap. This will make spreading the frosting much easier.

Petite Peppermint Cake

Makes 1 (6-inch) cake

Cake:
½ cup butter, softened
1 cup sugar
½ teaspoon vanilla extract
1⅓ cups all-purpose flour
1¼ teaspoons baking powder
½ cup whole buttermilk
2 egg whites, beaten until stiff

Frosting:
1 (4-ounce) bar white chocolate, chopped
2 tablespoons heavy whipping cream
6 tablespoons butter, softened
¼ cup sour cream
¼ teaspoon peppermint extract
3 cups confectioners' sugar, sifted
Garnish: peppermints, candy canes, or ribbon candy (see tip below)

1. To prepare cake: Preheat oven to 350°. Grease and flour 2 (6-inch) round cake pans; set aside.

2. In a medium bowl, beat butter and sugar at medium speed with an electric mixer until fluffy. Beat in vanilla.

3. In a medium bowl, sift together flour and baking powder. Gradually add to butter mixture alternately with buttermilk, beginning and ending with flour mixture. Fold in beaten egg whites, one-third at a time. Spoon batter into prepared pans. Bake for 28 to 30 minutes or until a wooden pick inserted in center comes out clean. Cool in pans for 10 minutes. Remove from pans, and cool completely on wire racks.

4. To prepare frosting: In a medium bowl, combine white chocolate and cream. Microwave on High in 30-second intervals, stirring after each, until chocolate is melted and smooth (about 1 minute total); let cool completely.

5. In a large bowl, combine white chocolate mixture, butter, sour cream, and peppermint extract. Beat at medium speed with an electric mixer until smooth. Gradually add confectioners' sugar, beating until creamy.

6. To assemble cake: Spread frosting between layers and on top and sides of cake. Garnish with candy, if desired.

One Cake, Two Ways

Perfect for a small gathering, our Petite Peppermint Cake is a tiny treat that you can garnish to suit the occasion. Dress it up for a fancy or formal affair with an elegant cake topper composed of ribbon candy. To complete the look, crush a few candy pieces for a decorative border around the bottom of the cake, and tie a shiny ribbon in a bow around the cake plate pedestal. When the occasion calls for something a bit more whimsical, try decorating the confection with miniature candy canes and party-staple peppermints. Children of all ages will delight in helping place the candies on the cake. Finish with a dusting of "snow" using Wilton's white cake sparkles (available at wilton.com and Michaels).

Apple Streusel Coffee Cake

Makes 10 to 12 servings

1½ cups finely chopped Granny Smith apple
½ cup raisins
½ cup chopped pecans
½ cup firmly packed brown sugar, divided
¾ teaspoon ground cinnamon, divided
½ cup butter, softened
½ cup sugar
¾ cup sour cream
2 large eggs
2 teaspoons vanilla extract
1½ cups all-purpose flour
1 teaspoon baking powder
½ teaspoon baking soda
¼ teaspoon salt
¼ cup toffee bits
½ cup confectioners' sugar
2 to 3 teaspoons milk

1. Preheat oven to 350°. Grease and flour a 9-inch round cake pan.

2. In a small bowl, combine chopped apple, raisins, pecans, ¼ cup brown sugar, and ½ teaspoon cinnamon; set aside.

3. In a medium bowl, combine butter, sugar, and remaining ¼ cup brown sugar. Beat at medium speed until fluffy. Add sour cream, eggs, and vanilla, beating until well combined.

4. In a small bowl, combine flour, baking powder, baking soda, and salt. Gradually add to butter mixture, beating until well combined.

5. Spread half of batter in prepared pan; sprinkle apple mixture over batter. Spread remaining batter over apple mixture; sprinkle with toffee bits. Bake for 45 to 50 minutes or until a wooden pick inserted in center comes out clean. Cool for 10 minutes; remove from pan, and cool completely.

6. In a small bowl, combine confectioners' sugar, remaining ¼ teaspoon cinnamon, and 2 teaspoons milk. Add additional milk if thinner consistency is desired. Drizzle over cooled cake.

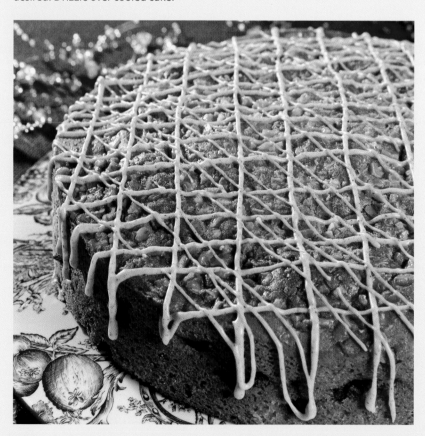

Ginger Pound Cake with Maple Glaze

Makes 1 Bundt cake

½ cup butter, softened
½ cup shortening
2 cups sugar
5 large eggs
½ cup milk
1½ teaspoons vanilla extract
2 cups all-purpose flour
1 tablespoon ground ginger
¼ teaspoon salt
½ cup confectioners' sugar
3 to 4 tablespoons maple syrup
1 teaspoon maple flavoring
Garnish: chopped candied ginger,
　　chopped pecans

1. Preheat oven to 300°. Grease and flour a Bundt pan.

2. In a large bowl, beat butter, shortening, and sugar at medium speed with an electric mixer until fluffy. Add eggs, one at a time, beating well after each addition. Add milk and vanilla, beating well.

3. In a small bowl, sift together flour, ginger, and salt. Gradually add to butter mixture, beating well to combine.

4. Spoon batter into prepared pan. Bake for 1 hour and 10 to 15 minutes or until wooden pick inserted in center comes out clean. Loosely cover with aluminum foil during last 20 minutes of baking to prevent excessive browning. Cool in pan for 10 minutes; remove to wire rack, and cool completely.

5. In a small bowl, combine confectioners' sugar, 3 tablespoons maple syrup, and maple flavoring. Add additional maple syrup if thinner consistency is desired. Drizzle over cooled cake. Garnish with ginger and pecans, if desired.

Pecan Cheesecake Bars

Makes 2 dozen

1½	cups all-purpose flour
1½	cups firmly packed brown sugar, divided
½	cup butter, softened
2	cups finely chopped pecans, divided
2	(8-ounce) packages cream cheese, softened
½	cup sugar
½	cup milk
2	teaspoons vanilla extract
½	cup light corn syrup
⅓	cup butter, melted
3	large eggs, lightly beaten

1. Preheat oven to 350°. In a medium bowl, combine flour and ¾ cup brown sugar. Using a pastry blender, cut in ½ cup butter until mixture resembles coarse crumbs. Stir in ½ cup pecans. Press mixture evenly in bottom of a 13x9-inch baking pan; bake for 10 minutes.

2. In a medium bowl, combine cream cheese and sugar; beat at medium speed with an electric mixer until smooth. Add milk and vanilla, beating until well combined; pour over cooled crust. Bake for 15 minutes; remove from oven, and cool for 10 minutes.

3. In a medium bowl, combine remaining ¾ cup brown sugar, corn syrup, melted butter, and eggs. Stir in remaining 1½ cups pecans. Pour over cream cheese mixture. Bake for 40 to 45 minutes or until center is set.

Chocolate-Hazelnut Biscotti

Makes about 2¹/₂ dozen

2½ cups all-purpose flour
1 cup sugar
2 teaspoons baking powder
½ teaspoon salt
1½ cups finely chopped hazelnuts
1 cup mini semisweet chocolate morsels
½ cup butter, melted and cooled
3 large eggs, beaten
1 teaspoon vanilla extract

1. Preheat oven to 350°. Lightly grease a baking sheet.

2. In a medium bowl, combine flour, sugar, baking powder, and salt. Add hazelnuts and chocolate morsels, stirring well.

3. In a separate bowl, combine butter, eggs, and vanilla. Add to flour mixture. Stir until dry ingredients are moistened; dough will be sticky.

4. On a lightly floured surface, shape half of dough into a 14x2-inch log; repeat with remaining dough. Place logs 3 inches apart on prepared baking sheet. Bake for 25 minutes or until set; remove from oven. Cool on pan for 10 minutes. Reduce oven temperature to 300°.

5. Cut each log crosswise into ¾-inch-thick slices with a serrated knife. Place slices, cut sides down, on baking sheet. Bake, turning slices every 10 minutes, for 30 minutes or until crisp and lightly browned on both sides. Remove from pan, and cool completely on a wire rack.

Coconut-Toffee Blondies

Makes 2 dozen

½   cup butter, melted
1½ cups sugar
½   cup firmly packed dark brown sugar
2   large eggs
2   teaspoons vanilla extract
1   teaspoon coconut extract
2   cups all-purpose flour
½   teaspoon salt
1   (3.5-ounce) can sweetened flaked
    coconut
½   cup toffee bits
Garnish: sifted confectioners' sugar

1. Preheat oven to 350°. Spray a 13x9-inch baking pan with nonstick baking spray with flour; set aside.

2. In a large bowl, combine butter and sugars. Beat at medium speed with an electric mixer until combined. Add eggs, vanilla, and coconut extract, beating to combine.

3. In a separate bowl, combine flour and salt; stir in coconut. Add to butter mixture, beating at low speed until blended. Press batter into prepared pan. Sprinkle evenly with toffee bits.

4. Bake for 20 to 25 minutes or until a wooden pick inserted in center comes out clean. Cool completely. Cut into squares, and sprinkle with confectioners' sugar, if desired.

Lemon Cheesecake Squares

Makes 2 dozen

2¼ cups all-purpose flour, divided
½ cup confectioners' sugar
1 cup butter, softened
½ cup finely chopped unsalted cashews
2 (8-ounce) packages cream cheese, softened
2¼ cups sugar, divided
½ cup milk
1 teaspoon lemon extract
4 large eggs
2 teaspoons lemon zest
⅓ cup fresh lemon juice
½ teaspoon baking powder
Garnish: confectioners' sugar, raspberries, lemon zest

1. Preheat oven to 350°. In a medium bowl, combine 2 cups flour and confectioners' sugar. Using a pastry blender, cut in butter until mixture is crumbly; stir in cashews. Press mixture evenly into bottom of a 13x9-inch baking pan; bake for 15 minutes.

2. In a medium bowl, combine cream cheese and ½ cup sugar; beat at medium speed with an electric mixer until smooth. Add milk and lemon extract, beating until well combined; pour over crust. Bake for 15 minutes; remove from oven, and cool for 10 minutes.

3. In a medium bowl, whisk together remaining 1¾ cups sugar, eggs, lemon zest, and lemon juice. In a small bowl, combine remaining ¼ cup flour and baking powder; add to sugar mixture, whisking to combine. Pour over cream cheese mixture.

4. Bake for 40 minutes or until a wooden pick inserted in center comes out slightly sticky. Cut into squares, and garnish with confectioners' sugar, raspberries, and zest, if desired.

Holiday Cherry Charlotte

Makes 1 (8½-inch) Charlotte

2	tablespoons sugar, divided
1	tablespoon cornstarch
2	(15-ounce) cans whole Bing cherries in juice, drained, ½ cup juice reserved
¼	cup cherry-flavored brandy, divided
2	(3-ounce) packages ladyfingers, split (about 46)
2	tablespoons cold water
2	teaspoons unflavored gelatin
1	(8-ounce) package cream cheese, softened
¼	cup unsalted butter, softened
1	cup confectioners' sugar
2	cups heavy whipping cream

Garnish: fresh mint leaves

1. In a medium saucepan, combine 1 tablespoon sugar and cornstarch. Gradually add reserved ½ cup cherry juice and 2 tablespoons cherry-flavored brandy, whisking until smooth. Bring to a simmer over medium heat, and cook for 1 to 2 minutes or until mixture is clear and thickened, stirring frequently. Remove from heat, and stir in cherries. Set aside to cool completely.

2. Line bottom of an 8½-inch springform pan with waxed paper. Lightly spray bottom and sides with nonstick cooking spray. Line bottom and sides of springform pan with ladyfingers.

3. In a small microwave-safe bowl, combine water and gelatin; let stand for 2 minutes. Microwave on High in 30-second intervals, stirring after each, until gelatin dissolves (about 1 minute total). Set aside to cool for 5 minutes.

4. In medium bowl, combine cream cheese, butter, and remaining 2 tablespoons cherry-flavored brandy. Beat at medium speed with an electric mixer until creamy. Gradually add confectioners' sugar, beating well.

5. In a separate bowl, beat cream and remaining 1 tablespoon sugar until soft peaks form. Add dissolved gelatin, and beat until stiff peaks form. Gently fold into cream cheese mixture.

6. Spoon into prepared pan. Arrange cherry mixture over filling, reserving a few cherries for garnish, if desired. Cover with plastic wrap, and chill for 4 hours or up to overnight. To serve, remove plastic wrap, and run a knife around edge of pan. Carefully unlatch ring, and remove. Garnish with mint and cherries, if desired.

Chocolate-Covered Almond Toffee

Makes 36 pieces, pictured on page 208

1	cup butter
1½	cups sugar
½	cup firmly packed light brown sugar
¼	cup water
2	tablespoons light corn syrup
1½	cups toasted sliced almonds, divided
1½	cups semisweet chocolate morsels
1	teaspoon shortening

1. Lightly spray 3 (12-cup) mini muffin pans with nonstick cooking spray; set aside.

2. In a large saucepan, melt butter over medium heat. Add sugars, water, and corn syrup, stirring well. Cook, stirring until sugar dissolves. Increase heat to medium-high. Bring mixture to a boil. Cook, stirring constantly with a wooden spoon, until a candy thermometer registers 300°. Remove from heat, and stir in 1 cup almonds. Working quickly, carefully spoon about 1 tablespoon mixture into each prepared muffin cup.

3. In a small bowl, combine chocolate morsels and shortening. Microwave on High in 30-second intervals, stirring after each, until melted and smooth (about 1½ minutes total). Spoon about 2 teaspoons chocolate mixture on top of sugar mixture in each cup, spreading chocolate to edges. Sprinkle remaining ½ cup almonds on top of chocolate. Let stand for 1 hour or until chocolate is set.

Double-Chocolate Éclairs

Makes 1 dozen

Pastries:
1   cup all-purpose flour
¼   teaspoon salt
1   cup water
½   cup butter
4   large eggs

Filling:
½   cup unsalted butter, softened
3   cups confectioners' sugar
¼   cup heavy whipping cream
4   (1-ounce) squares unsweetened
      baking chocolate, melted and cooled
1   tablespoon chocolate liqueur
      (optional)
½   teaspoon light corn syrup

Glaze:
⅔   cup heavy whipping cream
2   tablespoons sugar
2   tablespoons light corn syrup
¾   cup semisweet chocolate morsels

1. To prepare pastries: Preheat oven to
400°. Line a baking sheet with parchment
paper; set aside.

2. In a small bowl, sift together flour and
salt. In a medium saucepan, bring water and
butter to a boil over medium heat. Add flour
mixture, and stir vigorously with a wooden
spoon until mixture forms a ball. Remove
from heat; let cool for 10 minutes.

3. Add eggs, one at a time, to flour mixture,
beating with wooden spoon for 30 seconds
after each addition. Using a pastry bag
fitted with large round tip, pipe batter into
4-inch-long strips, 2 inches apart, on
prepared baking sheet.

4. Bake for 30 to 35 minutes or until golden
and puffy; cool on a wire rack. Cut off top of
each pastry, reserving top; pull out and
discard soft dough inside.

5. To prepare filling: In a medium bowl, beat butter at medium speed with an
electric mixer until creamy. Gradually add confectioners' sugar alternately with
cream; beat until light and fluffy. Add melted chocolate, chocolate liqueur, and
corn syrup, beating until well combined.

6. To prepare glaze: In a medium saucepan, bring cream, sugar, and corn syrup to
a boil over medium heat. Add chocolate morsels, stirring until chocolate melts and
mixture is smooth. Let cool slightly before using.

7. To assemble éclairs: Spoon or pipe filling into pastry bottoms. Dip pastry tops
in glaze, letting excess drip off; place tops on éclairs.

Lemon Meringue Pie

Makes 1 (9-inch) deep-dish pie

Crust:

1½	cups all-purpose flour
½	teaspoon salt
⅓	cup shortening
6	tablespoons cold water
½	cup white chocolate morsels
2	tablespoons heavy whipping cream

Filling:

1	cup sugar
¼	cup cornstarch
¼	teaspoon salt
1	cup water
4	egg yolks, lightly beaten
⅓	cup fresh lemon juice
2	tablespoons butter
2	tablespoons sour cream
1	tablespoon lemon zest
1	teaspoon vanilla extract

Meringue:

3	egg whites
¼	teaspoon cream of tartar
⅓	cup sugar

1. To prepare crust: In a medium bowl, combine flour and salt. Using a pastry blender, cut in shortening until mixture is crumbly. Add water, and stir just until moistened. Form into a ball, and wrap tightly in plastic wrap; refrigerate for 1 hour.

2. Preheat oven to 475°. On a lightly floured surface, roll pastry to a 12-inch circle. Place in a 9-inch deep-dish pie plate. Trim excess pastry ½ inch beyond edge of pie plate. Fold edges under, and crimp. Prick bottom and sides of crust with fork. Bake for 8 to 10 minutes or until lightly browned.

3. In a small microwave-safe bowl, microwave white chocolate and cream on High in 30-second intervals, stirring after each, until melted and smooth (about 1 minute total). Spread evenly over bottom of baked pie crust; set aside.

4. To prepare filling: In a medium saucepan, combine sugar, cornstarch, and salt. Gradually whisk in water. Bring to a boil over medium-high heat; cook for 1 minute, whisking constantly. Remove from heat.

5. Gradually add ½ cup hot sugar mixture to egg yolks, whisking to combine. Whisk yolk mixture into remaining hot sugar mixture in saucepan. Return to medium heat, and cook for 1 to 2 minutes, whisking constantly, or until mixture is thickened. Whisk in lemon juice, butter, sour cream, lemon zest, and vanilla. Cook for 1 minute or until mixture is thickened. Remove from heat.

6. To prepare meringue: In a medium bowl, beat egg whites and cream of tartar on high speed until foamy. Gradually add ⅓ cup sugar, beating until stiff peaks form.

7. Pour hot filling into baked pie crust. Spread meringue over hot filling, completely sealing to edge of crust. Bake for 20 minutes or until lightly browned. Cool at room temperature for 1 to 2 hours; chill before serving.

Apple-Pear-Cranberry Pie

Makes 1 (9-inch) deep-dish pie

Crust:

3	cups all-purpose flour
1	teaspoon salt
⅔	cup shortening
7	tablespoons cold water

Filling:

4	cups thinly sliced Granny Smith apple
3	cups thinly sliced green Anjou pear
1	cup dried cranberries
2	tablespoons fresh lemon juice
⅔	cup firmly packed brown sugar
¼	cup plus 1 tablespoon sugar, divided
¼	cup cornstarch
½	teaspoon ground cinnamon
¼	teaspoon ground nutmeg
⅛	teaspoon salt
1	tablespoon milk

1. To prepare crust: In a medium bowl, combine flour and salt. Using a pastry blender, cut in shortening until mixture is crumbly. Add water, and stir just until moistened. Divide dough into two balls. Wrap tightly in plastic wrap; chill for 1 hour.

2. Preheat oven to 350°.

3. To prepare filling: In a large bowl, combine apple, pear, cranberries, and lemon juice. Toss gently to coat. In a separate bowl, combine brown sugar, ¼ cup sugar, cornstarch, cinnamon, nutmeg, and salt. Add brown sugar mixture to apple mixture; toss gently to coat.

4. On a floured surface, roll half of pastry to a 12-inch circle. Place in a 9-inch deep-dish pie plate. Trim excess pastry ½ inch beyond edge of pie plate. Place apple mixture into prepared crust. Roll remaining pastry to ⅛-inch thickness. Using a pastry wheel or knife, cut into ½-inch-wide strips. Arrange in lattice design over apple mixture. Trim strips even with edges. Press edges together. Fold edges under, and crimp. Brush crust with milk, and sprinkle with remaining 1 tablespoon sugar.

5. Bake for 45 to 50 minutes or until lightly browned.

German Chocolate Pecan Pie

Makes 1 (9-inch) deep-dish pie

Crust:
- 1½ cups all-purpose flour
- ½ teaspoon salt
- ⅓ cup shortening
- 4 tablespoons ice water

Filling:
- 1 cup firmly packed light brown sugar
- ½ cup light corn syrup
- ½ cup dark corn syrup
- ¼ cup butter, melted
- 3 large eggs
- 1½ teaspoons vanilla extract
- ¼ teaspoon salt
- 2 cups pecan halves
- ¾ cup semisweet chocolate morsels
- 1½ cups sweetened flaked coconut

Garnish: whipped cream, chocolate curls, chopped pecans

1. To prepare crust: In the work bowl of a food processor, combine flour, salt, and shortening. Pulse until mixture resembles coarse crumbs. With processor running, add ice water through food chute, 1 tablespoon at a time, until mixture forms a ball. Flatten dough into a disk, wrap in plastic wrap, and refrigerate for 1 hour.

2. Preheat oven to 350°. On a lightly floured surface, roll pastry to a 12-inch circle. Fit pie crust into a 9-inch deep-dish pie plate. Trim excess pastry ½ inch beyond edge of pie plate. Fold edges under, and crimp. Cover bottom of pastry with pie weights. Bake for 8 minutes; remove pie weights, and set aside.

3. To prepare filling: In a large bowl, combine brown sugar and corn syrups. Add melted butter, eggs, vanilla, and salt; whisk until well combined. Stir in pecans. Sprinkle chocolate morsels evenly over bottom of prepared crust. Sprinkle coconut on top of chocolate morsels. Spoon brown sugar mixture on top of coconut.

4. Bake for 1 hour or until middle is set. If necessary, cover loosely with aluminum foil during last 10 minutes of baking time to prevent excessive browning. Cool completely. Garnish with whipped cream, chocolate curls, and pecans, if desired.

229

Easy Banana Pudding

Makes 12 servings

1 (5.1-ounce) box instant vanilla-flavored pudding mix
1 (3.4-ounce) box instant banana cream-flavored pudding mix
2½ cups milk
1 (8-ounce) container sour cream
1 (16-ounce) container frozen whipped topping, thawed
1 (12-ounce) box vanilla wafers
6 ripe bananas, sliced
Garnish: crushed vanilla wafers

1. In a large bowl, combine pudding mixes and milk; whisk until smooth. Add sour cream; stir until smooth. Fold in whipped topping.

2. In a large bowl, layer one-third of pudding mixture, half of vanilla wafers, and half of bananas; repeat layers. Top with remaining pudding mixture. Garnish with crushed vanilla wafers, if desired.

Strawberry Panna Cotta with Spiked Strawberry Sauce

Makes 6 servings

Panna cotta:
1 (0.25-ounce) envelope unflavored gelatin
2 tablespoons cold water
1 (16-ounce) container frozen sliced strawberries in syrup, thawed
1¼ cups heavy whipping cream
½ cup sugar
½ cup sour cream
1 tablespoon fresh lemon juice

Sauce:
Reserved strawberry puree
    (about 1½ cups)
½ cup sugar
1 tablespoon fresh lemon juice
2 tablespoons vanilla-flavored vodka
Garnish: fresh mint, sliced fresh strawberries

1. To prepare panna cotta: In a small bowl, combine gelatin and cold water; let stand for 5 minutes.

2. In the work bowl of a food processor, puree strawberries until smooth. Measure ½ cup strawberry puree; set aside. Reserve remaining strawberry puree (about 1½ cups) for sauce.

3. In a medium saucepan, combine cream and sugar over medium heat, stirring until sugar dissolves. Add gelatin mixture, stirring until gelatin dissolves. Remove from heat; whisk in ½ cup strawberry puree. Add sour cream and lemon juice, whisking until smooth. Pour into 6 (3x1½-inch) fluted molds. Refrigerate until slightly cool; cover surface with plastic wrap, and chill completely.

4. To prepare sauce: In a medium saucepan over medium heat, combine strawberry puree, sugar, and lemon juice. Bring to a simmer; cook for 6 to 7 minutes, stirring frequently. Remove from heat, and stir in vodka. Cool slightly. Cover and chill.

5. Carefully remove panna cotta from molds. Serve with sauce. Garnish with fresh mint and strawberry slices, if desired.

Mint Sorbet

Makes about 1 quart

3	cups water
1½	cups sugar
1	cup fresh mint leaves
3	tablespoons lime juice
2	tablespoons crème de menthe
2	tablespoons minced fresh mint leaves

Garnish: fresh mint sprigs

1. In a medium saucepan over medium-high heat, combine water, sugar, and 1 cup mint leaves. Cook for 10 minutes, stirring frequently to dissolve sugar; strain and cool completely.

2. In a medium bowl, combine syrup and remaining ingredients (except garnish). Place mixture in an ice cream freezer, and freeze according to manufacturer's instructions until firm; store in freezer in a freezer-safe container.

3. To serve, spoon sorbet into a bowl or glass, and garnish with mint sprigs, if desired.

Strawberry and Lavender Sorbet

Makes 5 cups

2	cups sugar
2	cups water
1	teaspoon dried lavender
2	cups sliced fresh strawberries
¼	cup fresh lemon juice

Garnish: fresh strawberries, dried lavender

1. In a medium saucepan over medium-high heat, combine sugar, water, and lavender. Cook for 10 minutes, stirring frequently to dissolve sugar; strain and cool completely.

2. In container of an electric blender or food processor, combine strawberries and lemon juice; process until pureed.

3. In a large mixing bowl, combine syrup and strawberry puree. Place mixture in an ice cream freezer, and freeze according to manufacturer's instructions until firm; store in freezer in a freezer-safe container.

4. To serve, spoon sorbet into a bowl or glass, and garnish with fresh strawberries and dried lavender, if desired.

Citrus Sorbet

Makes about 1 quart

2 cups sugar
2 cups water
1 tablespoon grated lemon zest
1 tablespoon grated lime zest
1 tablespoon grated orange zest
1½ cups fresh lemon juice
2 tablespoons fresh lime juice
2 tablespoons fresh orange juice
Garnish: lemon slices, lime slices, orange slices

1. In a medium saucepan over medium heat, combine sugar and water. Bring mixture to a boil; reduce heat to low, and simmer for 3 to 4 minutes, stirring constantly. Remove from heat, and cool completely.

2. In a large bowl, combine syrup and remaining ingredients (except garnish). Place mixture in an ice cream freezer, and freeze according to manufacturer's instructions until firm; store in freezer in a freezer-safe container.

3. To serve, spoon sorbet into a bowl or glass, and garnish with lemon slices, lime slices, and orange slices, if desired.

Watermelon Sorbet

Makes 1½ quarts

2 cups sugar
1 cup water
6 cups seeded and diced watermelon
2 tablespoons lime zest
½ cup fresh lime juice
¼ teaspoon salt
Garnish: lime zest, fresh mint

1. In a small saucepan, combine sugar and water over medium-high heat. Bring mixture to a boil; reduce heat to low, and simmer for 3 to 4 minutes, stirring constantly. Remove from heat, and cool completely.

2. In the work bowl of a food processor, puree watermelon until smooth. Strain juice through a fine-mesh strainer, pressing solids with the back of a spoon; discard solids.

3. In a medium bowl, combine sugar mixture, watermelon juice, lime zest, lime juice, and salt. Cover and chill for at least 4 hours or overnight. Pour mixture into a gel-type countertop freezer. Freeze according to manufacturer's instructions. (Sorbet will be soft.) Transfer to an airtight freezer-safe container. Freeze for at least 4 hours or overnight. To serve, spoon sorbet into a bowl or glass. Garnish with lime zest and mint, if desired.

235

ACKNOWLEDGEMENTS

Over the years, we have been blessed by the generosity and hospitality of many homeowners as well as by our friends at some of the finest stores and companies in the world. To them, we offer our sincerest gratitude for help with the contents of this special volume of collected recipes.

Annieglass

Anthropologie

At Home Furnishings

Bed Bath & Beyond

Beverly Ruff Antiques and Linens

Brach's

The Briarcliff Shop

Bromberg's

Crate and Barrel

Earthborn Pottery

Flora Bella

Gien

Hallmark

Harmony Landing

Hobby Lobby

HomeGoods

Iron Art Inc.

The Iron Fish

John Toole

Juliska

Kmart

Kim Seybert

Lowe's

Macy's

Mariposa

Michaels

Mulberry Heights Antiques

The Nest

The Optima Company

Pier 1 Imports

Pottery Barn

Ralph Lauren Home

Saks Fifth Avenue

Seibels

Smith's Variety

Stein Mart

Summerhill, Ltd.

Sweet Peas Garden Shop

Table Matters

Target

Tricia's Treasures

Victoria Trading Co.

Vietri

Waterford

Whole Foods

Williams-Sonoma

Wisteria

World Market

RECIPE INDEX